Goodness & Advice

THE UNIVERSITY CENTER
FOR HUMAN VALUES SERIES

AMY GUTMANN, EDITOR

Goodness & Advice

JUDITH JARVIS THOMSON

PHILIP FISHER

MARTHA C. NUSSBAUM

J. B. SCHNEEWIND

BARBARA HERRNSTEIN SMITH

Edited and Introduced by

AMY GUTMANN

PRINCETON UNIVERSITY PRESS
PRINCETON AND OXFORD

Library of Congress Cataloging-in-Publication Data

Thomson, Judith Jarvis.
Goodness and advice / Judith Jarvis Thomson ; edited and
introduced by Amy Gutmann.
p.   cm. — (The University Center for Human Values series)
Includes bibliographical references and index.
ISBN 0-691-08673-7 (alk. paper)
1. Ethics.   2. Consequentialism (Ethics)
1. Gutmann, Amy. II. Title.   III. Series.
BJ1012 .T545 2001
170—dc21   00-048322

This book has been composed in Janson Text

The paper used in this publication meets the minimum requirements of
ANSI/NISO Z39.48-1992 (R 1997) (*Permanence of Paper*)

www.pup.princeton.edu

Printed in the United States of America

1   3   5   7   9   10   8   6   4   2

CONTENTS

INTRODUCTION

Amy Gutmann

How should we live? What do we owe to other people? How, if at all, do ethical demands and prudential ones differ? Is there any moral difference between our actions (such as killing) and inactions (such as letting die) when each has the same consequences (the loss of a life)? Judith Jarvis Thomson is a contemporary moral philosopher who has not avoided such big questions. At one time or another in her distinguished career, she has addressed each of these questions, and she continues to do so in her 1999–2000 Tanner Lectures on Human Values at the University Center for Human Values at Princeton University.

This book consists of Thomson's revised Tanner Lectures, with commentaries by Philip Fisher, Martha Nussbaum, Jerome Schneewind, and Barbara Herrnstein Smith, along with a reply by Thomson to her commentators. Thomson's arguments show the value—as well as the limits, which all modes of intellectual inquiry have—of trying to answer big moral questions by a scrupulous mode of philosophical inquiry. The commentaries give prominent voice to recurrent claims about the limits of such philosophical inquiry, which Thomson then addresses in her reply to commentators.

Some kinds of philosophical reasoning about questions such as "What ought I to do?" seem peculiar, even wrongheaded, to many people. Fisher and Herrnstein Smith give voice to such criticism. Instead of using real-world examples in all their empirical complexity and ambiguity, Thomson tends to offer seemingly simple, hypothetical examples, taken out of context. Why? By using hypothetical examples, she tries to determine whether some widely held philosophical generalizations are—as they claim—generally defensible.

In Part I, on "goodness," she tests the popular and intuitively appealing moral claim: "Act always to bring about the most good in the world." To test this moral generalization, she employs some simple examples that are presented (at first) totally out of context. "Alfred presses the doorbell." Should he do so? In light of such examples, she asks, can we coherently and credibly stand by the claim "Act always to bring about the most good in the world"? Ironically, Thomson uses such simple examples, taken out of context, to arrive at a conclusion with which she is in heated agreement with those who challenge her use of such examples. All agree—although for different reasons and by employing very different methods and styles of argument—that it is a mistake to generalize about what actions are good apart from a context that raises the questions "Good in what way?" "For whom?" "Under what circumstances?"

Some contemporary moral philosophers not only address big questions about the nature of ethical action, but also try to come to conclusions about controversial ethical issues in their writings. They move beyond hypothetical problems to actual ones. They do not shy away from some of the most controversial ethical problems of our time, such as abortion, affirmative action, and physician-assisted suicide. Thomson is also one of these philosophers. She has dared to defend the morality of abortion, affirmative action, and physician-assisted suicide, with important qualifications that come out of her careful analysis of examples, both hypothetical and actual. While some philosophers have opened themselves to criticism for using seemingly trivial or bizarre hypotheticals, and other philosophers have opened themselves to criticism for stepping beyond the bounds of "value-free" inquiry for taking morally controversial positions on actual issues, Thomson has repeatedly done both. She has demonstrated the courage of her philosophical and moral convictions. In this volume, she defends the idea that the two kinds of convictions—philosophical and moral—go hand in hand. In the realm of moral philosophy, she argues, philosophical claims are not one thing and moral claims another, and never the twain shall meet.

The aim of Thomson's inquiry—an aim that she shares even with many who disagree with the conclusions that she reaches—is to examine what it takes to answer the question: "What should I do in this situation?" Thomson asks, "Should I act always to bring about the best consequences?" The attraction of answering "yes" is a single simple principle that tells us what we should do in any given situation: Always act in a way to bring about the best consequences! People who subscribe to this principle are called Consequentialists. Thomson then reminds us: To know how one should act as a good Consequentialist, one needs to be able to answer the question "What are the best consequences?"

Some Consequentialists are called Classical Utilitarians because they follow Jeremy Bentham, who argued that good consequences are those that produce pleasure, and bad consequences are correspondingly those that produce pain. According to Benthamite Utilitarianism, we should always act in a way to maximize the net amount of pleasure (over pain) in the world. The idea that morality requires people to bring about the greatest amount of good—meaning pleasure—in the world has been a very appealing and at times extremely progressive doctrine. Few philosophers have been more effective than Bentham in directly helping to bring about progressive political reforms on the basis of his philosophy. He championed penal reform in nineteenth-century

England, for example, by invoking his Utilitarian philosophy to oppose the infliction of unnecessary pain on prisoners.

The Utilitarian source of progressive penal reform is also the source of some less appealing or apparently progressive points of view. What does Utilitarianism have to say, for example, about people who enjoy the suffering of others? Some people who enjoy the suffering of others may try to bring about more suffering in the world, and that would be bad from a Utilitarian perspective. But what about those people who do not try to bring about more suffering in the world, but simply take pleasure in the suffering of other beings? Thomson thinks that taking pleasure in someone else's suffering is adding something bad to the world, not something good. One can think this without denying that a person's enjoyment adds to the net amount of pleasure in the world. It is bad, Thomson suggests, for a person to enjoy the suffering of others even when he cannot do anything to relieve that suffering. She faults Utilitarianism for being incapable of appreciating—let alone accepting—this judgment. Utilitarianism's response is to remind us that pleasure is good and pain is bad. But is pleasure always good? Not, Thomson thinks, when the pleasure consists in being pleased at someone else's suffering.

Thomson therefore objects to what she calls "Hedonism About Goodness," an idea at the heart of Classical Utilitarianism. Hedonism About Goodness is the idea that an event is good to the extent that it is pleasurable to sentient beings. Stated this abstractly, hedonism about pleasure is intuitively appealing to many people. But its appeal diminishes when we consider a person who takes pleasure in the pain of other sentient beings. The person does not cause other people pain—which Utilitarianism would also count as bad—but rather he simply takes pleasure in pain that he cannot ameliorate. The Utilitarian reasoning is that it is good to add pleasure to the world, and therefore to the extent that we cannot ameliorate the pain of others, we might as well take pleasure in it. Thomson suggests why criticism of people who take pleasure in the pain of others makes moral sense. "There is a world of difference," she writes, "between pleasures according as their objects differ from each other." If the object of our pleasure is the singing of Jessye Norman, then our pleasure is good; but if the object of our pleasure is the torturing of prisoners of war, then our pleasure is bad. This is so even if we have no power to effect any change in either the singing or the torturing.

This basic criticism of Utilitarianism is the beginning of a far-ranging critique by Thomson that extends beyond Utilitarianism to the more general moral perspective called Consequentialism. Consequentialism is not committed to Hedonism About Goodness, but it is committed to the principle that people should act always to bring about the best consequences. Consequentialism can reject Hedonism About Goodness. It therefore need not approve of people getting pleasure out of the pain of other sentient beings. So why then criticize Consequentialism? The idea that we ought to act so as to bring about the best consequences is very appealing on its face.

Consequentialism, according to Thomson, has another, closely related problem, which arises precisely because it rejects Hedonism About Goodness. Consequentialism needs to offer an account of what events are good and what events are bad. It must offer such an account because it must be able to say what it means to bring about the best consequences. After all, the core of Consequentialism—its very defining doctrine—is the requirement that people should act in such a way as to bring about the best consequences. So if we are to defend Consequentialism, we must know what it means to bring about the best consequences.

Thomson's most striking claim in Part I, on "goodness," is that the seemingly simple and appealing advice that people should act "to bring about the best consequences"—or, what is the same, to bring about the most good—is meaningless. Thomson argues that Consequentialism must ultimately fail because its basic requirement—that people bring about the "most good"—has no meaning. Good is always good in some way, in some context, for some beings.

To make this claim about the meaninglessness of the "good" less abstract, Thomson asks us to consider a question like the following: Is drinking (whole) milk good? We can't answer this or any other question about what is "good" when it is posed so abstractly. Why? Because to make the question meaningful we need to consider *the ways* in which something may be good. Drinking milk may be good or bad, but only in different ways. Drinking milk is good for women who need calcium (and have low cholesterol), and bad for men who have high cholesterol (and don't need calcium). It is not simply good or bad (full stop).

What this and many other examples tell us, according to Thomson, is that the moral command "Act in a way so as to bring about the most good" is meaningless. Since there is no such thing as good, simply and strictly speaking, there can be no such thing as being morally required to bring about the most good in the world. It is therefore not so much wrong as it is meaningless to say that people should act so as to maximize goodness in the world. There are too many different ways in which actions can be good or bad to make the idea of maximizing goodness meaningful.

Thomson rejects what she calls Moorean Consequentialism for this reason. In her commentary, Nussbaum suggests that more recent conceptions of Consequentialism are immune from Thomson's critique. The conception proposed by the political philosopher Philip Pettit or the economist Amartya Sen, for example, does not ask people to act so as to maximize goodness in the world. "Sensible" Consequentialism does not presuppose a unitary conception of the good. What does it then advise us to do? Pettit's conception asks us to choose our actions on the basis of relevant consequences. Sen asks us to choose our actions on the basis of the probable states of affairs brought about by our actions. Sensible Consequentialism seems to stand up to Thomson's critique because it explicitly admits that there are many different ways in which the consequences of our actions can be good and bad.

But Thomson says that Sensible Consequentialism cannot succeed simply by admitting that there are many different ways in which consequences can be good and bad. It needs to do more than reject a unitary conception of the good. Pettit's Sensible Consequentialism needs to tell us how first to choose which consequences are relevant, and then to decide which of the relevant consequences to pursue. Sen's Sensible Consequentialism needs to tell us how to evaluate and compare the various states of affairs that our actions (or inactions) can bring about. All kinds of Sensible Consequentialism need to give us a way to answer the question "What should we do in this situation?" Furthermore, they need to answer the question exclusively on the basis of the consequences of the alternative actions that are open to us. (If they admit a consideration other than consequences, then they cease to be distinctively Consequentialist theories.) Sensible Consequentialism therefore needs to give us guidance in how comparatively to evaluate the relevant alternative consequences, or states of affairs, that our actions can produce.

In reply to Nussbaum, Thomson makes yet another striking claim: Sensible Consequentialism has no future. Why? Without a unitary conception of the good, Consequentialism has no credible and consistent way of ranking alternative outcomes. Should you give money to a needy friend, to Oxfam, buy yourself a luxurious dinner, or flush the money down the toilet? All of these alternatives—even flushing it down the toilet—can be good in some way. (Thomson discusses a few of the ways.) If Sensible Consequentialism diverges from Moorean Consequentialism by its rejection of ranking the different ways in which these alternatives can be good, then it cannot tell us what to do based on consequences only. Sensible Consequentialism admits other considerations besides consequences—such as our right to live our own life and our obligations to others. We then can rely in part (although not entirely) on these other considerations to aid us in deciding what to do.

But if Sensible Consequentialism welcomes non-Consequentialist considerations, it ceases to be a distinctive type of ethical theory. It is not, strictly speaking, Consequentialist. (Consequentialism strictly speaking counts only consequences.) How can Sensible Consequentialism—which considers more than consequences—be distinguished from sensible deontology—which considers rights and obligations but not only rights and obligations? Both take into account consequences, rights, and obligations, depending on what is at stake in an action. What, then, if anything, is the difference between Sensible Consequentialism and deontology? Do they simply—or, more accurately, *complexly*—converge?

Here and in her many other writings, Thomson is a critic of Consequentialism, strictly speaking. She offers an alternative way of thinking about morality. The consequences of our actions matter, but consequences are not all that matter. We also have our own lives to lead, and what we ought to do is therefore at least partly independent of whether our actions will produce good consequences in the world. Thomson's moral perspective takes seriously our distinctiveness as individuals. She therefore defends individual rights and their correlative obligations. According to Thomson, we have strict obligations to refrain from harming others even if such obligations sometimes mean that we should let harm be done rather than act so as to harm others. This claim— precisely because it can advise individuals not to harm others even when more harms will therefore be done—is controversial in a way that Consequentialism is not. Thomson never claims otherwise. She therefore continues to develop and defend her perspective against an impressive range of critics, some of them quite sympathetic yet unconvinced that she has answered all the important questions raised by one of the more promising moral perspectives of our time.

Schneewind raises one such question that any moral perspective should answer. Does knowledge of the moral "ought"—what we should do, morally speaking—bring with it the kind of necessity to act whether or not a divine lawgiver commands morality? Seventeenth-century natural law theorists presupposed a divine lawgiver and thought that the moral ought therefore was absolutely binding on everyone. Natural law theorists did not take the moral ought as "advice" but rather as "command." And not just any command, but the highest and most obligatory command, that of an omniscient and omnipotent God.

When morality is detached from a divine lawgiver, what changes? Does the way that people are bound by morality change, and if so, in what way and with what consequences? Thomson can only begin to answer this question in her reply to Schneewind. Even if the way people are (objectively) bound by morality does not change, as Thomson suggests, is the way that they (subjectively) think they are bound by morality likely to change when they no longer believe in God? "I greatly doubt," Thomson says, "that your moral views would be affected *just* by your shifting from the thought that God makes morality to the thought that morality makes itself." Her emphasis on the "just" is critical. Our metaphysics of morality, as she writes, "*can* leave everything the same." Yes, but is it *likely* that taking away God leaves people thinking that they are as bound by morality as they would otherwise think they are (or would actually be)? And if there are other things that tend to change with taking away God, how morally significant are those changes on people's desire to discern morality? On their motivation to act morally?

Is it the case that absent belief in God, more people tend to think—mistakenly, on Thomson's view—that they are not so bound by morality as they would otherwise be? This change—contingent as it is on human psychology—would in itself constitute a significant change in our moral world from that of the seventeenth century. Or is it the case that people who do not believe in God still think that they are every bit as bound by morality as people who believe in God? Or if not every bit as bound, still bound enough that the difference is one of degree, not of kind. And why do believers and nonbelievers (in God) think one way or the other, or vary even among themselves? Since believers and nonbelievers of many different kinds coexist, side by side, interdependently in our world, we should be able to find out how much of a difference belief makes. These would be fascinating findings, relevant to—but not determinative of—philosophical thinking about morality in our time. These are several of the many questions about morality that Thomson and her commentators urge us to pursue from different perspectives.

Goodness & Advice

JUDITH JARVIS THOMSON

Part One: Goodness

1.

TWENTIETH-CENTURY Anglo-American moral philosophy has been dominated by concern about the fact-value gap. Or at least about what appears to be a gap, indeed, an unbridgeable gap, between fact and value. Matters of fact seem to be epistemologically intelligible: we find out about them by the familiar methods of observation and experiment. Matters of value seem to be quite different. If we can't learn about them by reasoning to them from matters of fact, then there seems to be no way at all by which we can come to learn about them. But what reasoning could possibly take a person from a matter of fact to a matter of value? It is hard to see how any reasoning could. Are we therefore to conclude that nobody has good reason to believe about any judgment of value that it is true? Many moral philosophers regard that as an appalling conclusion, and try to show that it is unwarranted. Others

Delivered as a Tanner Lecture on Human Values at Princeton University, 1999. Printed with permission of the Tanner Lectures on Human Values, a Corporation, University of Utah, Salt Lake City, Utah.

What follows is a revised and expanded version of the lectures. I am grateful to my four commentators, and to the participants in the discussions following the lectures, for very helpful comments and criticism. Some of their comments have been taken into consideration in revising the text.

Material in Part I, sections 9–14, was part of a paper presented in a symposium with Dennis Stampe at the meeting of the American Philosophical Division, Central Division, in May 1999. I thank Stampe and the other participants for their comments and criticism.

think it the correct conclusion, and try to show that we should not be troubled by it. In any case, all start from the apparent fact-value gap; responding to the threat it seems to pose became the central task of Anglo-American moral philosophy in the century just past.

That there does not merely seem to be, that there really is a fact-value gap, is by now part of the culture. Or at least, part of a certain culture, that of the middle-class literate public. I don't need to *introduce* my freshmen to the fact-value gap: they bring it to college with them.

I do not mean that members of the public at large, and my college freshmen, do not have moral beliefs. Their acceptance of the idea that there is a fact-value gap shows itself in more subtle ways. If I ask my students whether it is morally permissible for people to lie and cheat whenever it would profit them to do so, they reply, "No, of course not." If I go on to ask what they would say if a man disagreed, they do not reply, "He's mistaken, for the following reason: . . . "—giving a reason. What emerges is rather: "It's all just a matter of opinion. I have mine and he has his, and they differ." Or: "It's all just a matter of how you feel. I feel one way, he feels another."

We might describe the situation in this way. People have a great many beliefs about what it is good or bad, right or wrong to do; these are their first-order moral beliefs. What many people lack nowadays is the second-order belief that they have good reason to believe that their first-order moral beliefs are true.

I suppose that in some people, lack of this second-order belief shows itself in lack of confidence in their first-order moral beliefs. I doubt that this is true of many people, however. For the most part, I think, people who think that there is an unbridgeable fact-value gap, and therefore conclude that nobody has good reason to believe about any value judgment that it is true, feel entirely confident that lying and cheating are wrong. In most people, I think,

4

lack of the second-order belief shows itself only on occasions on which they step back from ordinary life and reflect on their first-order moral beliefs—as, for example, in classrooms that say "Philosophy" on the door.

So where's the harm in it? I said just above that many moral philosophers regard the conclusion that nobody has good reason to believe about any judgment of value that it is true as appalling. Why so?—if accepting that conclusion is compatible with feeling entirely confident that lying and cheating are wrong.

That these are compatible is something that moral philosophers who accept the conclusion try to demonstrate. Perhaps they are right. Presumably it is not literally inconsistent in a man to feel entirely confident that a certain number will win tomorrow's lottery while believing that he has no good reason to believe it will. At best, however, he has a divided consciousness. And it would plainly be silly in him to stake much on that number.

Do those who accept the conclusion that nobody has good reason to believe about any judgment of value that it is true, while nevertheless feeling entirely confident that lying and cheating are wrong, have a divided consciousness? And would it be silly in them to stake much on its being the case that lying and cheating are wrong? These are good questions. But the prior question is surely whether anyone should accept that conclusion.

We should go back further, in fact. *Is* there really an unbridgeable gap between fact and value?

The prevalence of the idea that there is such a gap must have deep sources outside philosophy. That there is such a gap is a philosophical thesis, and no philosophical thesis becomes part of the culture unless there are other ideas in the culture that it reinforces and is reinforced by.

The prevalence of the idea that there is an unbridgeable gap between fact and value is overdetermined; in addition to sources outside philosophy, it has sources in other areas of philosophy as well as within moral philosophy. What I refer to are the grounds for a quite general skepticism that were laid out so strikingly by Descartes. My freshmen bring that too to college with them: they say that of course they believe they have fingers and toes, but they also say "That's just my opinion" and "That's just how I feel."

What I will fix on in Part I is one of the considerations within moral philosophy itself that has led moral philosophers to regard the idea as at a minimum having to be taken seriously. I will suggest that the consideration I discuss is a product of illegitimate abstraction.

2.

Since well before the twentieth century, moral philosophers have taken it to be their task to produce a theory about what we ought to do and why. That "why" is important: moralizers are happy to tell you what you ought to do—moral philosophers differ in that they aim to tell you also what makes it the case that you ought to do the things they say you ought to do. Moral philosophy, in other words, responds to the desire that moral requirement be 'rationalized', that is, shown to be a requirement.

Very well: what might be thought to make it the case that Alfred in particular, or people generally, ought to do this or that?

Suppose that Alfred acted in a certain way—he took off his hat, or pressed a certain doorbell, or what you will. Let us say he pressed a doorbell. For him to do that was for an event to occur, namely, the event that consisted in his pressing the doorbell.

We may suppose that Alfred's pressing the doorbell caused many other events to occur. Thus, his pressing the doorbell caused a circuit to close, a bell to ring, a person inside the house to feel pleased, and so on and on. These events—Alfred's pressing the doorbell, the circuit's closing, the bell's ringing, and so on—are all of them events that would not have occurred if Alfred had not pressed the doorbell.

More generally, for a person to act is for a battery of events to occur, events that would not have occurred if he had not acted. We could put it more grandly: for a person to act is for the world to go in a way that it otherwise would not.

If that is what it is for a person to act, then it is very natural to think that the question whether he ought to act in such and such a way must turn on a comparison between what the world will be like if he acts in that way and what the world will be like if he acts in any of the other ways in which it is open to him to act. So, for example, that the question whether Alfred ought to press the doorbell turns on a comparison between what the world will be like if he presses it and what the world will be like if he instead stamps his feet, or dances a jig, or stands stock still, or . . . There seems to be nothing else for it to turn on.

And what are the terms of the required comparison? An answer that all but suggests itself is this: we need to settle whether what the world will be like if he acts in such and such a way is *better or worse than* what the world will be like if he acts in any of the other ways in which it is open to him to act. Thus if the world will be better if Alfred presses the doorbell than it will be if he instead stamps his feet, and better than it will be if he instead dances a jig, and so on, then he ought to press the doorbell. And if the world will not be better if Alfred presses the doorbell than it will be if he instead does one of those other things, then it is not the case that he ought to press the doorbell.

In sum, a person ought to do a thing if and only if the world will be better if he does it than if he does any of the other things it is open to him to do at the time. Similarly, a person ought not do a thing if and only if the world will be worse if he does it than if he does any of the other things it is open to him to do at the time.

What if there is a tie? For example, what if the world will be equally good whether Alfred presses the doorbell or dances a jig, but better if he does either than if he does anything else it is open to him to do? The idea we are looking at yields that it is not the case that Alfred ought to press the doorbell and that it is not the case that he ought to dance a jig (since the world will not be better if he does either). But the idea also yields that it is not the case that Alfred ought not press the doorbell, and that it is not the case that Alfred ought not dance a jig (since the world will not be worse if he does either). So the idea yields that he need not, but may, do either. It also yields, however, that he ought not do anything other than either.[1] These conclusions are plausible enough, and the possibility of ties therefore does not constitute a difficulty for those who are attracted by this idea.

Following current usage, I will call the idea Consequentialism.[2] It is, I think, deeply satisfying. How *could* it be perfectly all right to do a thing if the world will be worse if you do it than if you do something else instead? Moreover, given that for a person to act just is for the world to go in a way that it otherwise would not go, surely the question whether he ought to act had better turn on a comparison between how it will go if he acts and how it will go if he does something else—to repeat, there seems to be nothing else for it to turn on. And how is that comparison to be made if not by settling on which way of going would be better?

---

[1] These are G. E. Moore's conclusions about ties; see his *Ethics* (London: Oxford University Press, 1949), 22–25. I thank Martha Nussbaum for reminding me of the need to mention ties.

[2] The idea was first given this name by G. E. M. Anscombe, in "Modern Moral Philosophy," *Philosophy* 33 (1958). Her article was reprinted in G. E. M. Anscombe, *Collected Philosophical Papers*, vol. 3 (Oxford: Basil Blackwell, 1981). The name is unfortunate, and more's the pity that it has become common usage, since it is so very likely to mislead. A Consequentialist does not believe that what fixes whether a person ought to do a thing is a comparison between the consequences of his doing it with the consequences of his doing anything else, if "consequences" is understood in the most natural way, namely as "effects." A Consequentialist believes that what fixes whether a person ought to do a thing is rather a comparison between what the world will be like if he does it with what the world will be like if he does anything else. These are very different ideas. For more on the difference, see note 3 below.

Down the road from this idea lies the fact-value gap, among other serious difficulties. I have wanted first to bring out the idea's attractions. It is not surprising that so many people have found it attractive, and that those who reject it do not merely dismiss it, but feel the need to make a case against it.

I stress that Consequentialism says nothing at all about what would make the world be better or worse than it otherwise would be. The idea itself leaves that open.

But a moral philosopher needs to arrive at a view about this, so let us turn to it.

3.

What would make it the case that the world will be better if a person does one thing than it will be if he does another? "Better" is just the comparative of "good," so we can re-put our question as follows: what would make it the case that the world will be more good if a person does one thing than it will be if he does another? It is very natural to think that the world will be more good if it contains more of what is good or less of what is bad or both. Consider Alfred again. I invited you to suppose that if Alfred presses the doorbell, a great many events will occur that otherwise would not, namely, his pressing the doorbell, the circuit's closing, the bell's ringing, someone's feeling pleased, and so on. We may similarly suppose that if Alfred instead dances a jig, a great many events will occur that otherwise would not. Will the world be better, that is, more good, if he presses the doorbell than if he dances a jig? That—it is very natural to think— turns on whether some or other of the events that will occur if he presses the doorbell, and some that will occur if he instead dances a jig, will be good or bad, and if so, on how good or bad they will be.

Which events are good and which bad? A familiar idea says that an event is good just in case it consists in someone's feeling pleased, and bad just in case it consists in someone's feeling pain. This idea comes down to us from Bentham and John Stuart Mill.

It is certainly possible for Jones to be more pleased than Smith is. Suppose that is now the case. If an event is good if and only if it consists in someone's feeling pleased, then presumably the event that consists in Jones's being pleased is better than the event that consists in Smith's being pleased. Similarly for pains: if Jones's pain is more severe than Smith's, then the event that consists in Jones's feeling pain is worse than the event that consists in Smith's feeling pain.

I will call this idea about which events are good or bad, and about how good or bad they are, Hedonism About Goodness. Many people have found it a very attractive idea.

To return to Alfred, then. If he presses the doorbell, a battery of events will occur. If he instead dances a jig, a different battery of events will occur. Hedonism About Goodness tells us which of those events are good and which bad, and how good or bad they are. I mentioned that if Alfred presses the doorbell, a person inside the house will be pleased. Suppose that if Alfred instead dances a jig, then Alfred will be pleased. Suppose that Alfred will be less pleased if he dances a jig than the person inside the house will be if Alfred presses the doorbell. That counts in favor of its being the case that the world will be better if he presses the doorbell than if he dances a jig. But of course we would need to know a good deal more if we were to arrive at a conclusion on this matter: we would need to know whether anyone else will be pleased if Alfred acts in each way, and moreover, whether anyone will feel pain if he does, taking into consideration everyone who would be affected by Alfred's pressing the doorbell and by Alfred's instead dancing a jig.

Still, if we conjoin Hedonism About Goodness with Consequentialism, we have produced a theory about what a person ought to do and why. A person ought to do a thing if and only if—and if so, *because*—the balance of pleasure and pain that ensues if he does it is greater than that which ensues if he does any of the other things it is open to him to do instead.

The idea we have reached is, of course, Utilitarianism. Utilitarianism is one version of Consequentialism: a Consequentialist is also a Utilitarian if and only if he accepts Hedonism About Goodness.[3] I have laid out the process of reasoning by which it may be reached at some length, in order to bring out that it relies on two ideas, which it is important to distinguish from each other. One is Consequentialism, the other is Hedonism About Goodness. The contemporary literature of moral philosophy is full of objections to Utilitarianism; it is important, however, to be clear which of those two ideas a given objection to Utilitarianism is an objection to.

I am going to focus on an objection to Consequentialism that I think has not been taken seriously enough. But let us begin with Hedonism About Goodness.

I tried to make Hedonism About Goodness seem plausible when I presented it, which from this vantage point—the end of

---

[3] I said in note 2 above that the following two ideas are very different: (i) what fixes whether a person ought to do a thing is a comparison between the effects of his doing it with the effects of his doing anything else, and (ii) what fixes whether a person ought to do a thing is a comparison between what the world will be like if he does it with what the world will be like if he does anything else. And I said that it is (ii), not (i), that a Consequentialist opts for.

The difference between those ideas emerges clearly only if a Consequentialist rejects Hedonism About Goodness. Suppose a Consequentialist accepts Hedonism About Goodness. Then on his view, what matters to the question whether Alfred ought (as it might be) to press the doorbell is only the effects of Alfred's doing so and the effects of Alfred's acting otherwise. For example, while if Alfred presses the doorbell, then the world will contain the event that consists in his pressing the doorbell, that morally irrelevant, since the event that consists in his pressing the doorbell is not itself, but at most has among its effects, events that consists in someone's being pleased or feeling pain.

But a Consequentialist might reject Hedonism About Goodness. In particular, he might instead say that some acts are themselves good or bad. On his view, then, it is not only events that are the effects of an act that matter morally, and opting for (ii) may yield a moral conclusion that is different from the moral outcome yielded by (i).

the twentieth century—is not easy to do. I know of no moral philosophers nowadays who accept it. Among many other objections, it has often been pointed out that a man might be pleased at someone else's feeling pain. Is his feeling pleased really to be thought a good event? We are surely inclined to think it positively vicious in a person to take pleasure in the pains of others. Insofar as we have intuitions about what counts as a good event— and I will return to this caveat shortly—it strikes us, intuitively, that a man's feeling pleased at the pain of another is not a good event.

Moreover, there is an interplay between Hedonism About Goodness and Consequentialism. Suppose we accept Consequentialism. If we were also to accept Hedonism About Goodness, then we would be committed to supposing that it counts in favor of the conclusion that we ought to do a thing that our doing it will cause a man to feel pleased at the pain of another—and indeed, counts the more strongly in favor of this conclusion, the more pleased he will be. We may well think that must be wrong.

Well, I will be suggesting that we should reject Consequentialism, so the fact that if you accept it, you had really better not also accept Hedonism About Goodness does not strike me as a serious objection to Hedonism About Goodness. What is objectionable about Hedonism About Goodness is internal to it. Feeling pleased is feeling pleased *by* something, and there is a world of difference between pleasures according as their objects differ from each other.

So suppose we reject Hedonism About Goodness. If we wish to retain Consequentialism, we now have a problem on our hands.

4.

A serious problem. For which events are good and which bad? What answer to this question is to replace Hedonism About Goodness? Suppose my team plays your team in the football finals, and that my team wins. "That's good," I say. "That's bad," you say. Which of us is right? How on earth is that question to be answered?

It might be suggested that neither of us is right—that is, that the event of my team's winning is not itself either good or bad, that, as some philosophers would say, the event of my team's winning is not *intrinsically* good or bad. Rather, it is at most *instrumentally* good or bad, good or bad only insofar as the events it will cause are intrinsically good or bad. Which, then, are the intrinsically good or bad events?

We might try to construct some examples. Suppose Alfred aims a gun at Bertha and fires it; Alfred misses, however, so Bertha survives. Perhaps we can say that Bertha's survival is an intrinsically good event. Bertha's death, had that occurred, would have been an intrinsically bad event; fortunately, her death did not occur.

There is a difficulty here, however, analogous to the one I pointed to when we looked at Hedonism About Goodness. For what if the reason why Alfred was aiming his gun at Bertha is that Bertha was villainously trying to kill Alfred? Let us suppose that Bertha, having survived, now kills Alfred, just as she had been villainously trying to. Are you still sure that Bertha's survival was an intrinsically good event? And that her death would have been an intrinsically bad one?

We might well want to say that a person's surviving—whether or not the person is a villain—is good for him, and that his death would be bad for him. But we need to remember that an event that is good or bad for one person can be the opposite, namely bad or good, for another person.

It has to be remembered also that what is in question here is not whether an event is good *for* or bad *for* a person, but rather whether it is just plain good or just plain bad. That is our question. And it is not in the least clear how it is to be answered.

13

5.

But what is good or bad for people must surely be in some way relevant to whether a person ought to act. Perhaps what is good or bad for people itself fixes what is just plain good or just plain bad? Perhaps a Consequentialist should therefore opt for the following idea about goodness: one event is better than another if and only if the first is 'more better for more' than the other. Consider again the event that consists in my team's winning its game with yours. "That's good," I say. "That's bad," you say. I asked: which of us is right? Perhaps the answer to this question is to be found out by finding out how many people the event is good for and how many it is bad for, and how good it is for those it is good for, and how bad it is for those it is bad for—the answer to the question being an appropriate function of those facts.

A Consequentialist who likes this idea could then say: the world will be better if a person does such and such than it will be if he does anything it is open to him to do instead just in case his doing the such and such will be more better for more. And if it will be, then it follows that that is what he ought to do.

There is a difficulty for this view that is a first cousin of one we have met twice before. Suppose it would profit me a lot to make you suffer a minor loss; suppose also that no one else would be affected by my act. It follows on this view that I ought to make you suffer the loss. That can't be right. There may well be cases in which it is permissible, even morally required, that one person cause another a loss. But it can't at all plausibly be thought that the mere fact that I would gain more by acting than you would lose counts in favor of its being the case that I ought to act.

The Consequentialist who rejects this idea about goodness can of course reject this outcome. He can remind us that he did not say that what matters morally is what is more good for more: what he said is that what matters morally is what is more good. And he can declare that some events that are more good for more may perfectly well be bad events. In particular, an event that consists in taking advantage of another for one's own profit may well be a bad event even if it is more better for more than any alternative open to the agent at the time.

It pays to stress this point. It seems nigh on a necessary truth that what a person ought to do is what would make the world be best—more good—than any alternative. That is why Consequentialism seems so attractive. It takes only a moment's reflection to see that it is not only not a necessary truth but false that what a person ought to do is what would make the world be more better for more than any alternative.

Of course a Consequentialist who rejects this idea about goodness owes us a better one. And what might that be?

6.

To summarize where we have come so far. I drew attention in section 4 to the attractiveness of Consequentialism, which is the idea that a person ought to do a thing if and only if the world will be better if he does it than if he does anything else it is open to him to do instead. And we were supposing that whether the world will be better turns on a comparison between the goodness or badness of the events that will occur if he does or does not choose the option. But which events are good and which bad? Once we have cut ourselves loose from Hedonism About Goodness, and from the idea I described in the preceding section, we are out at sea, adrift. It would be no surprise if people found themselves wondering how anyone could be supposed to have good reason for believing that a person ought to act in this way or that.

The point may be put another way. According to Consequentialism, the concept 'ought' reduces to the concept 'good'. If you want to know whether someone ought to do a thing, you need to ask what events will occur if he does it and what events will occur if he does anything else, and whether those events will be good or bad, and if so, how good or how bad. Let us now distinguish between two ways in which it can seem that we are at risk of having to become skeptics about morality. The first is this: it may be said that we just can't find out what all the events are that will occur if a person does or does not do a thing. Consider again Alfred's pressing the doorbell. I mentioned some of the events that that event will cause, but there are surely indefinitely many others that it will also cause. If we don't know which they all are, we can't even begin to assess the goodness or badness of all of them, and therefore can't find out whether Alfred ought to press the doorbell. I will call this shallow skepticism about morality. It is skepticism *about morality* because it is skepticism about the possibility of finding out what Consequentialism says must be found out if we are to find out whether judgments about what people ought to do are true. But it is shallow skepticism about morality because it is ultimately skepticism about matters of fact. The shallow skeptic says that if we could find out about the relevant matters of fact, then finding out about what people ought to do would be no problem.

Some Consequentialists have been shallow skeptics about morality, and contentedly so. I have G. E. Moore in mind in particular. According to Moore, we must just hope for the best: if we manage to do what we ought to do, that is just good luck for us. Other Consequentialists have not been contented at the prospect of having to become shallow skeptics about morality. No matter for our purposes.

For what we have in fact reached is the prospect of something markedly more worrisome, namely deep skepticism about morality. What we have reached is that even if we knew about all the events that will occur if a person acts and all that will occur if he does not, we are still in epistemological trouble because we have found no satisfactory way of settling which of those events would be good and which bad. What looms is the fact-value gap, and it looks unbridgeable.

So what's to be done?

7.

I suggest that the reason why we find no satisfactory way of answering the question which events are good and which are bad is that there is no such question. Consequentialism requires that there be such a question, and that we be able to answer it if we are to be able to tell whether a person ought to do a thing. That, I suggest, is itself a conclusive objection to Consequentialism.

If someone draws our attention to a certain event—say, Alfred's pressing a certain doorbell—and asks us whether that was or would be a good event, or a bad event, or neither, we should not think "Ah, what a hard question"; we should instead ask ourselves whether we so much as understand what we have been asked.

Why do we think we do understand? Or anyway, why do so many moral philosophers think they do? One answer emerges clearly in G. E. Moore's *Principia Ethica*, with which twentieth-century Anglo-American moral philosophy began.

Moore said it is clear that some things are good, some are bad, and some are neither. Goodness, he said, is the property that all and only the good things have in common. That is the property that we would be ascribing to a thing—whether an event or anything else—if we said of it "That's good"; and that is the property such that we are asking whether a thing possesses it when we ask about the thing "Is it good?"

This idea seems to issue from nothing better than an oversimplified conception of the way in which the adjective "good" functions in English. When people say about a thing "That's good," what they mean is always that the thing is *good in some way*. Perhaps they mean that the thing is a good fountain pen. Or a good book. Or a good apple. If so, what they mean is that the thing is good of a kind.

There is more too. A person might say "That's good," not meaning that the thing is good of a kind, but that it is good for use in doing this or that. Perhaps that the thing is good for use in making cheesecake. Or they may mean that the thing is good *for* such and such or so and so. Perhaps that the thing is or would be good for Alfred, or for England, or for the tree in my backyard. Or they may mean that the thing tastes good or looks good.

When talking about a person, they may say "He's good," meaning by this that he's good at playing chess, or that he is morally good—just or honorable or generous. When talking about an experience or an activity, they may say "It's good," meaning by this that it's pleasant or enjoyable.

What people *say* is the words "That's good," or "He's good," or "It's good," but what they mean—what *they*, but not their words, mean—is that the thing is good in one or other of the kinds of ways I have indicated.[4] It is the context in which they assert those words that makes clear what they meant by the words, that is, what, perhaps given their preceding remarks, their hearers are entitled to suppose they mean. If the context does not make this clear, then their hearers are at a loss.

We should be clear that the ways in which a thing can be good that I have been indicating are not *grounds* for thinking a thing is good. St. Francis was good. How so? Well, he was a morally good person—he was just and kind. Chocolate is good. How so? Well, it tastes good. If what I have supplied you with are grounds for thinking that St. Francis and chocolate are good, that is, grounds for thinking that they both possess the property goodness, then it ought to be in order to ask which is better, for the adjective

---

[4] This is a point I have made in a number of other places, most recently in "The Right and the Good," *Journal of Philosophy* 94, no. 6 (June 1997).

"good" has a comparative. But do you make sense of the question whether St. Francis was better than chocolate?

I think we had better conclude that there is no such property as goodness. All goodness, as we can put it, is goodness in a way. When it is asked whether a thing is good—whether the thing is a book or pie tin, or a person or an event—the context, or the speaker, needs to let us in on what the relevant way of being good is, or we not only can't answer the question, we don't even know what question was asked.

Consider events in particular. Suppose someone asks whether Alfred's pressing the doorbell is or would be a good event. We should reply "How do you mean? Do you mean 'Would it be good *for* somebody?'" And we had better be told whether that is what is meant, or whether something else is meant. We had better not be told that what is in question is instead whether the event is just plain, pure good, for there is no such thing.

8.

Consequentialism, then, has to go. What is to replace it is a hard question, the harder in that Consequentialism rests on ideas that are very attractive. I will concentrate on it in Part II. Meanwhile, however, it pays to take note of some things we gain if we reject the question whether or not a thing is plain, pure good.

Most important, we are not now confronted with an unbridgeable fact-value gap.

For in the first place, there is no one fact-value gap: if there is one, there are many. Suppose we know a lot of facts about a certain fountain pen: how much ink it will hold, that it does not leak, how smooth its nib is, and so on. Ah, but is it a *good fountain pen*? Again, suppose we know a lot of facts about what a certain event would cause. Let it be the event that consists in Alfred's drinking some hot lemonade. Suppose, then, that we know, in particular, what that event would cause, given the condition Alfred is cur-rently in—as it might be, that he has a sore throat. Ah, but would Alfred's drinking some hot lemonade be *good for him*? Again, sup-pose we know a lot of facts about how a certain brandy tastes: austere and delicate. (I take this description from a *New York Times* article on brandies.) Ah, but does the brandy *taste good*? If there are fact-value gaps, then I have drawn attention to three of them, for it is not at all plausible to think that what we have here are three cases in which we have facts in hand, and need to be told what consideration—the same in all three—would take us from the facts to the values. Whatever it is, if anything, that would entitle us to pass from those facts about the fountain pen to the conclusion that it is a good fountain pen is not at all plausibly thought to be the same as what would entitle us to pass from facts about Alfred and hot lemonade to the conclusion that his drink-ing some would be good for him, or the same as what would entitle us to pass from facts about how the brandy tastes to the conclusion that it tastes good.

Second, we should ask whether there really are unbridgeable fact-value gaps in the cases I mentioned.

What facts about a fountain pen warrant concluding that it is a good fountain pen? Well, some things are clear. It mustn't leak, it must be sturdy, it must hold enough ink to write several pages before filling, its nib must be smooth so as not to tear the paper being written on. A good fountain pen is one that would serve well the typical purposes of those who want fountain pens. And whether a pen would serve those purposes well is something we can and do find out all the time.

If Alfred has a sore throat, then it is very likely that the event that consists in his drinking some hot lemonade would be good for him. Why so? Well, it is very likely that his drinking some will make him feel better. Of course, that might be mistaken. Perhaps he has an ulcer as well as a sore throat; then, perhaps, drinking hot lemonade would not make him feel better, and would in fact be bad for him. We know perfectly well what *kinds* of consideration bear on the question whether that event would be good for him. There certainly are cases in which it is hard to find out whether an event would be good for a person, and among them are cases in which we may have to conclude that we cannot find this out. Perhaps we are unable to attach weights to the various considerations that bear on whether the event would be good for him, as, for example, where the event consists in his making this or that choice among possible careers. Still, there are limits to what counts as a consideration in such cases.

Whether something tastes good is a messier matter. That is partly due to the fact that we have so little in the way of phenomenological characterizations of tastes—getting past "sweet," "sour," "bitter," and "salty" is, for most of us, rather a stretch. It takes a professional to describe a brandy as austere and delicate. Moreover, most of us do not really attend to tastes very closely, and do not notice in them what a professional notices.[5] When you think on how important the tastes of things are to us, that can seem very surprising. The questions that arise here are interesting and, I think, insufficiently studied by philosophers. For our purposes, however, it is perhaps enough to draw attention to the fact that there is a difference, which is plain to all of us, between a person's *liking* the taste of something and its tasting good. Lots of people like the taste of strawberry Kool-Aid: it sells very well indeed. For all that, strawberry Kool-Aid does not taste good.[6]

---

[5] More from the *Times* article about another brandy: it is "round and notably spicy in flavor, with hints of nutmeg, cinnamon and hazelnuts." J. L. Austin asked—in *Sense and Sensibilia*, ed. G. J. Warnock (Oxford: Oxford University Press, 1962)—"What sort of reception would I be likely to get from a professional tea-taster, if I were to say to him, 'But there can't be any difference between the flavors of these two brands of tea, for I regularly fail to distinguish between them'?" He left it to us to supply the answer.

[6] There is a term that I think appropriate here. Lots of people like what can best be described as kitsch. Kool-Aid is kitsch in the realm of taste.

There are ways of being good that are of particular interest to the moral philosopher, and I will be returning to them in Part II. Meanwhile, it just is not in general true that our intellectual lives are everywhere crisscrossed by unbridgeable fact-value gaps. The adjective "good" is among the most commonly used in the English language. What we should have been doing is to look at how it is in fact used, and at what does in fact settle that it is or is not applicable.

9.

A further benefit can be got by attending to the ways of being good. There is a concept which has been much leaned on by many contemporary moral philosophers, but which has seemed very dark to others. What I refer to is the concept 'reason for a person to do such and such'. It has been thought to have an intimate connection with the concept 'ought'. Some philosophers hold that it is not the case that a person ought to do a thing unless there is a reason for him to do it. Or even more strongly: what a person ought to do is precisely what there is most reason for him to do. I leave aside for the time being the question how the concept 'ought' connects with the concept 'reason for acting'. Let us ask instead what must surely be the prior question: what *is* a reason for a person to do such and such?

It is easy enough to begin: a reason for a person to do a thing is something that counts in favor of his doing it. But what is that?[7]

---

[7] T. M. Scanlon says:

> Any attempt to explain what it is to be a reason for something seems to me to lead back to the same idea: a consideration that counts in favor of it. "Counts in favor how?" one might ask. "By providing a reason for it" seems to be the only answer.

And Scanlon therefore says he will take the concept of a reason as primitive. See his *What We Owe to Each Other* (Cambridge: Harvard University Press, 1998), 17. As will emerge in section 12 below, I think there is another, better because more informative, answer to the question what it is for X to count in favor of a person's doing a thing than that X is a reason for the person to do it.

There are a number of answers in the literature—I will discuss two of them.

Before we turn to them, however, we need to adopt two regimentations. The need for the first issues from the existence of a scatter of locutions in which the term "reason" appears: we need to decide how to connect the most common of them.

The weakest is the kind I started with, an example of which is:

(1) There is a reason for Alfred to press the doorbell, namely X.

I take it that (1) is consistent with Alfred's not believing that X is a reason for him to press the doorbell. Indeed, I take (1) to be consistent with Alfred's believing that there is no reason at all for him to press the doorbell.

There is room for dispute about what is the actual, or anyway the most common use of

(2) Alfred has a reason for pressing the doorbell, namely X.

For simplicity, I bypass arguments about usage. I will take it that Alfred can't have a reason for pressing the doorbell unless there really is one. Thus I will take it that (2) entails (1). On the other hand, I will also take it that it can't be the case that Alfred has a reason for pressing the doorbell, namely X, unless Alfred believes that X is a reason for him to press the doorbell. Thus I will take it that although (2) entails (1), (2) is not entailed by (1). I think that this decision does capture the most common use of (2), but whether it does does not matter for our purposes.

Suppose Alfred is now in process of pressing the doorbell. We may say:

(3) Alfred's reason for pressing the doorbell is X.

I take (3) to be stronger than (2). Alfred can have a reason for pressing the doorbell, namely X, and nevertheless not press it.

(Perhaps he has a better reason for not pressing it.) By contrast, X can't be Alfred's reason for pressing the doorbell unless he is pressing it for that reason, and thus unless he is in fact pressing it. So (3) entails (2), but (3) is not entailed by (2).

So (3) is stronger than (2), and (2) is stronger than (1). I think that no theoretical issue turns on these decisions about (1), (2), and (3); that is why I say that what is in question here is (mere) regimentation.

Similarly for reasons for believing, or wanting, or expecting, or regretting, or hoping for, or feeling angry at, or . . . a thing; thus for anything for which there might be, and a person might have, a reason.

The need for a second regimentation is due to the fact that we need to fix on a general characterization of what a reason *is*. What, after all, might X be?

A reason is something one might reason *from*. What might a person reason from? Suppose that Alfred believes that Bertha's pig can fly. Why? Suppose the situation is this: Alfred believes that all pigs can fly, and therefore concludes that Bertha's pig can. We have three options.

(i) We can say that Alfred's reason for believing that Bertha's pig can fly is the fact that he, Alfred, believes that all pigs can fly. While pigs can't fly, Alfred does anyway believe that they can.

I think it plain that this option is not a happy one. Alfred does not reason that Bertha's pig can fly from the fact that he, Alfred, believes that all pigs can. His reasoning, we are supposing, went like this: "All pigs can fly, therefore Bertha's pig can." His premise was not that he, Alfred, believes that all pigs can fly, but rather that all pigs can fly.

I am not suggesting that a person couldn't reason to a certain conclusion from the fact that he believes this or that. That does seem to be possible. Suppose that Charles has loved Dora for years, but his suit had always seemed hopeless. He is now suddenly struck by the thought that Dora loves him too. He concludes—from the very fact that he now believes she does—that there must have been some evidence of her love for him in her past behavior, evidence that was unrecognized by him at the time, and is still unclear to him now. Cases in which a person reasons to a conclusion from the fact that he believes this or that must surely be rare, however: normally, we reason not from our believing something, but rather from what we believe.

I did not spend time on option (i) because I think it a plausible description of Alfred: I did so because an analogue of the point I make here will reappear later.

A second possible description of Alfred, (ii), is that his reason for believing that Bertha's pig can fly is the proposition that all pigs can fly. That proposition is false, but we could say never mind: Alfred thinks it true, and reasons from it to his conclusion. More generally, we can say that a reason is always a proposition, true or false, which someone who thinks it true might reason from; and where a person thinks a proposition is true and reasons from it, *it* is *his* reason.

The third possible description of Alfred, (iii), is that Alfred has no reason for believing that Bertha's pig can fly. This is what we say if we take it that a reason is always a fact. Alfred might himself say "My reason for believing that Bertha's pig can fly is the fact that all pigs can fly." If that is what he says, then it is clear that although he thinks he has a reason for believing that Bertha's pig can fly, he doesn't actually have one, since there is no such fact as the fact that all pigs can fly.

It should be noticed that opting for (iii) is compatible with supposing that there is an answer to the question why Alfred believes that Bertha's pig can fly. We can say that he believes that Bertha's pig can fly because he believes that all pigs can. In other words, we can explain his believing that Bertha's pig can fly. We cannot explain his believing that Bertha's pig can fly by giving his reason for believing it, since, according to (iii), he hasn't any; but he believes that all pigs can fly, and though that belief of his is false, the fact that he has it, we can say, is why he believes that Bertha's pig can fly.

I think that no deep theoretical issue turns on a decision between (ii) and (iii), for I think that any interesting claim we make about reasons on the supposition that they are propositions has an equally correct or incorrect analogue about reasons on the supposition that they are facts. That is why I take it, once again, that what is in question here is (mere) regimentation. Since taking reasons to be facts seems to me to square with usage better than taking them to be propositions, I will take them to be facts.

It should perhaps be stressed: I will be taking it that a reason is a fact not merely where it is a reason for believing something, but also where it is a reason for doing something. Indeed, also where it is a reason for feeling something or for wanting something and so on—that is, for whatever it is that a reason might be a reason for.

So much for regimentation. I said at the beginning of this section that a reason for a person to do a thing is something that counts in favor of his doing it. Given our second regimentation, we can re-put this point as follows: a reason for a person to do a thing is a fact that counts in favor of his doing it. Which facts are those? I said I would discuss two answers that may be found in the literature.

10.

According to the first answer, every reason for action is a desire, or want.[8] Suppose that Alfred wants to please Bertha. Suppose also that his pressing a certain doorbell would please her. Then,

[8] What I describe here is a simplified version of the theory argued for by Dennis Stampe in "The Authority of Desire," *Philosophical Review* (July 1987).

on this view, there is a reason for Alfred to press the doorbell, namely his wanting to please Bertha. What makes his wanting to please her a reason for him to press the doorbell is the fact that his pressing it would please her; but that being a fact, his wanting to please her *is* a reason for him to press it.

Given our first regimentation, it can of course be the case that although

> (1) There is a reason for Alfred to press the doorbell, namely his wanting to please Bertha,

is true,

> (2) Alfred has a reason for pressing the doorbell, namely his wanting to please Bertha,

is false—after all, he may not know that his pressing the doorbell would please Bertha, and therefore not know that his wanting to please Bertha is a reason for pressing it. But if he does know that his pressing the doorbell would please her, and therefore believes that his wanting to please her is a reason for pressing the doorbell, then (2) is true. And we can understand how that reason counts in favor of his ringing the doorbell: it makes his ringing the doorbell be attractive to him.

This view is entirely compatible with our having bad reasons for action. Suppose instead that Alfred wants to annoy Bertha, and that his pressing the doorbell would in fact annoy her. Then there is a reason for him to ring the doorbell, namely his wanting to annoy Bertha. If he knows these things, then he has a reason for pressing the doorbell—and the reason counts in favor of his pressing the doorbell in that it makes his pressing the doorbell be attractive to him. That outcome is as it should be, for any theory of reasons for action must allow for the possibility of, indeed the fact of, there being bad reasons for action as well as good ones.

The theory also allows for there being stronger or weaker reasons for action: this difference (it says) turns on the strength or weakness of the want.

Given our second regimentation, however, this won't quite do as it stands. A desire is presumably a mental state. For example, and more precisely: Alfred's wanting to please Bertha consists in his being in a certain mental state. Alfred's wanting to annoy Bertha consists in his being in a different mental state. Is his being in a mental state a fact? Surely not: that idea seems to be a category mistake.

If a person's wanting something consists in the person's being in a certain mental state, then it looks as if no desire is a reason for action, since no desire is a fact.

An emendation all but suggests itself. A friend of this first theory could say that a reason for action is not itself a desire, but is instead the fact that consists in the person's having the desire.[9] Thus the reason there is for Alfred to press the doorbell is the fact that Alfred wants to please (or annoy) Bertha. And it is that—that fact—that makes his pressing the doorbell be attractive to him.

But the theory still won't do. As I said earlier, a reason is something a person might reason *from*. There surely are cases in which a person reasons to something from the fact that he wants something. In particular, there are cases in which a person takes the fact that he wants something to be a reason for doing something. Suppose Carol has always disliked milk in the past. She now finds herself wanting to drink some. There is a theory according to which people's wants in food often issue from a nutritional deficiency, thus, for example, that wanting to drink some milk might issue from a need for calcium. Let's suppose that theory is true,

---

[9] Stampe agrees that a reason is a fact, and he tells us that when he says that a desire is a reason for action, what he really means is this: the fact that the person wants something is a reason for the person to act accordingly. See ibid.

and that Carol believes it is. Then she might think: "Here is an interesting fact I have just noticed about myself: I want to drink some milk. Wanting to drink milk sometimes issues from a need for calcium. Therefore I may well need some calcium (which milk supplies). So my wanting to drink some milk is a reason for me to drink some." This is probably a relatively rare kind of case, however: normally, we reason not from the fact that we want something, but rather from facts about what we want and how it might be got.

Carol, who takes the fact that she wants to do something to be a reason for doing it, should remind us of Charles, who takes the fact that he believes one thing to be a reason for believing another. Both kinds of case are surely rare.

If so, then we cannot suppose that every reason for action is a desire. At most some are.

11.

I said that I would discuss two answers to the question what facts are reasons for action. Fortunately we can be brief about the second.

On this second view, every reason for action is a combination (a pair? a conjunction?) of a desire and a belief.[10] Suppose that Alfred wants to please Bertha and believes that his pressing a certain doorbell would please her. Then, on this view, there is a reason for Alfred to press the doorbell, namely the combination consisting of his wanting to please Bertha and his belief that his pressing it would please her. Moreover, Alfred has a reason for

---

[10] An influential example is Donald Davidson's account of reasons for action in "Actions, Reasons, and Causes," *Journal of Philosophy* 60 (1963). That article was reprinted in his *Essays on Actions and Events* (Oxford: Oxford University Press, 1980). According to Davidson, any pro-attitude can play the role of the required desire. Friends of this theory, and it has a great many, do not typically trouble themselves over the question what the mode of combination is, and I leave it open.

pressing the doorbell, namely that want/belief combination—which counts in favor of his pressing the doorbell since it makes doing so be attractive to him.

We can, as I said, be brief about this theory. Given our second regimentation, a reason is a fact, so we had better reconstrue the theory to say that a reason for acting is not a want/belief combination but rather a combination consisting of the fact that a person wants this and the fact that he believes that. A reason, however, is something that one might reason from. But as we know, it is rare for a person to reason to something from the fact of his wanting this, and rare for a person to reason to something from the fact of his believing that—remember the cases of Carol and Charles—and presumably therefore at least as rare for a person to reason to something from the fact of his wanting this *and* believing that.

Why are so many philosophers inclined to say that a reason for acting is a want/belief combination? I think it pretty clear why they do. First, they think that a person's reason for doing a thing explains his doing of it.[11] Why so? It seems very plausible to think that if Alfred is pressing a doorbell for a reason, then when we have found out what his reason was, we have found out why he pressed it. That is, we have found an explanation of his pressing it. Indeed, what we have found, namely his reason for pressing the doorbell, itself explains his pressing it.

Following Hume, as many contemporary philosophers do, we may well believe, second, that something explains a person's doing a thing only if it contains a want and a belief. Something explains Alfred's pressing the doorbell only if it contains a want and a belief, in particular, the want and belief because of which he pressed it.[12]

---

[11] That this motivates the theory emerges clearly in Davidson, "Action, Reasons, and Causes." I hazard a guess that it also motivates the theory offered in Stampe, "The Authority of Desire."

[12] Hume did not, and contemporary philosophers also do not, say that something ex-

It follows that a person's reason for acting contains a want and a belief: a reason for acting is a want/belief combination.

This won't do, however. Following Hume, what explains a person's doing a thing is his wanting this and believing that. But the fact that he wants this and believes that is not likely to be his reason for doing the thing: such cases are rare. The more usual case is like this. We ask Alfred why he is pressing the doorbell, and he replies: "to please Bertha." We find out from his saying this that he wants to please Bertha, and believes that his pressing the doorbell will please her. And that—the compound fact that he wants to please Bertha and believes that his pressing the doorbell will please her—does explain his pressing the doorbell. But that compound fact is not his reason for pressing it.

This is why we can find out why a person does a thing even if he has no reason for doing it, but only thinks he does. Consider, first, reasons for belief. I invited you to imagine that Alfred believes that Bertha's pig can fly. We ask him why he believes this, and he says "All pigs can fly." According to our second regimentation, Alfred has no reason for believing that Bertha's pig can fly since there is no such fact as the fact that all pigs can fly. But we can nevertheless explain his believing that Bertha's pig can fly: he believes this because he believes that all pigs can.

So similarly for reasons for action. Suppose we ask Alfred why he is pressing a certain doorbell, and he replies: "to please Bertha." But suppose that his pressing the doorbell will not in fact please Bertha; suppose it will instead annoy her. Then Alfred has

---

plains just anyone's doing just anything only if it contains a want and a belief: on their view, this holds only of doings that are intentional. (If a man is nervously and unwittingly tapping his fingers, then it may be that there is no want and belief out of which he is doing it; and his doing of it is presumably explainable by appeal to something else, perhaps in a case such as this, to anxiety.) On the other hand, a person who does a thing for a reason does do it intentionally, and it is only doings of things for reasons that concern us here. I therefore omit the qualification.

no reason for pressing the doorbell. But we can nevertheless explain his pressing it: he is doing so because he wants to please Bertha, and believes that his doing so will please her.

12.

So what is a reason for doing a thing? It is something that counts in favor of doing it. Given our second regimentation, we can re-put this point as follows: a reason for a person to do a thing is a fact that counts in favor of his doing it. Which facts are those? We have now rejected two answers that may be found in the literature.

I suggest that it would pay us to help ourselves to the fact that all goodness is goodness in a way, and to consider the following sufficient condition for a fact to be a reason for a person to do a thing: a fact is a reason for a person to do a thing if it is a fact to the effect that his doing the thing would be good in some way.[13] There is a reason for Alfred to press that doorbell if his pressing it would be good for him. Or good for Bertha or Charles. Or would be enjoyable. (I suppose a person might like pressing door-bells.) And so on. And I suggest that it is clear that a fact to the effect that Alfred's pressing the doorbell would be good in some way counts in favor of his pressing it.

The fact that Alfred's pressing the doorbell would be good in some way may not everywhere count very strongly in favor of his pressing it: its being enjoyable to ring doorbells does not count very strongly in favor of pressing yours or mine. But the fact that doing so would be enjoyable does count in favor of doing so.

Moreover, Alfred has a reason for pressing the doorbell if, for some way of being good, W, he knows that his pressing the door-

---

[13] G. E. M. Anscombe said that a bit of practical reasoning must be understood to have a major premise that attributes what she called a "desirability characterization" to the act contemplated. See her *Intention* (Oxford: Basil Blackwell, 1957). I suggest that we can interpret her as meaning that the major premise must assert that the act would be good in some way.

bell would be good in way W. His knowing that pressing it would be good in way W is, of course, entirely compatible with his not pressing it. For example, he might not care in the least about the fact that his pressing the doorbell would be good in way W. But suppose he does care: suppose, in particular, that he wants to do something that is good in way W, and, in fact that he wants to do something that is good in way W more than he now wants to do anything else. Then given that he also believes that his pressing the doorbell would be good in way W, he may be expected to press it.[14] If he does press it, then his reason for pressing it is the fact that his doing so would be good in way W; and his wanting to do something good in way W, together with his believing that pressing the doorbell is good in way W, explains his pressing the doorbell.

It is perhaps worth stress that Alfred can believe that his pressing the doorbell would be good in a way W compatibly with (i) his not wanting to press it, and (ii) his not wanting to do something good in way W. That his believing that his pressing the doorbell would be good in way W is compatible with (i), his not wanting to press it, is probably obvious enough. Even if his belief is that his pressing the doorbell would be good for him. I may know that my taking a certain nasty-tasting medicine would be good for me without wanting to take it. If I do take it, then that is presumably because, given that taking it would be good for me, I am willing to take it; but being willing to take it is not the same as wanting to take it. I hope it is also obvious that Alfred's believing that his pressing the doorbell would be good in way W is compatible with (ii) his not wanting to do something good in way W. Even if the way of being good is goodness for him. I may refrain from taking the nasty-tasting medicine, not merely because it tastes bad, but because I do not now want to do what is good for me.

---

[14] I do not say that he will press it: I say only that he may be expected to do so, since I wish to leave room for the possibility of weakness of will.

The fact that one can know that doing a thing would be good in a certain way compatibly with wanting neither to do the thing nor to do something good in that way is due to the fact that it is *goodness in a way* that we are dealing with. A number of philosophers have held that believing a thing would be pure good, intrinsically good, motivates the believer to try to bring it about.[15] In particular, then, they have held that believing that one's doing a thing would be good motivates one to do it. Other philosophers have disagreed. Given the illegitimate abstraction that issued in the idea that there is such a property as goodness, and the consequent unclarity about what the property is, it is perhaps no surprise that this disagreement resists resolution.

In sum, I suggest that it would pay us to consider the following sufficient condition for a fact to be a reason for a person to do a thing: a fact is a reason for a person to do a thing if it is a fact to the effect that his doing the thing would be good in some way. Indeed, I think it a very plausible idea.

13.

There is a possible objection: accepting that sufficient condition yields that for each of the many things you might now do, there probably is at least one reason for you to do it. That is because there are many ways of being good, and for each of the many things you might now do, there probably is at least one way in which your doing it would be good. Your mowing my lawn would be good for me. Your watering my lawn would be good for me and it would also be good for my lawn. Suppose your neighbor is

---

[15] See, for example, Charles L. Stevenson, "The Emotive Meaning of Ethical Terms," *Mind* 46 (1937), reprinted in his *Facts and Values* (New Haven: Yale University Press, 1963). J. L. Mackie's reason for suspicion of the property goodness is the very fact—he takes it to be a fact—that if there were such a property, it would have to be a property such that believing that a thing would have it motivates the believer to try to bring the thing about. See his *Ethics: Inventing Right and Wrong* (London: Penguin Books, 1977).

doing something illegal; your helping him to hide the traces might be good for him. Again, your going out to dance a jig in the street might be good for use in a list (currently being compiled) of eccentric behaviors in the suburbs. And so on. But (so the objection goes): that many reasons for doing that many things is too many.[16]

My own impression is that this is not a worrisome objection. A reason for doing a thing counts in favor of doing it; but there being a fact that counts in favor of your doing a thing is entirely compatible with its being of no interest to you that there is. There being such a fact is also compatible with its being wrong for you to do the thing.

Moreover, any of the facts to the effect that your doing a thing would be good in a way might be your reason for doing it. As I say, you might not care that your doing a thing would be good in way W. But you might care; and it might be that you therefore do the thing for that reason.

It could of course be insisted that a fact to the effect that your doing a thing would be good in way W is a reason for you to do it only if you want to do what would be good in way W. Thus suppose you don't care that your watering my lawn would be good for me; suppose what you care about is lawns—what you want is that *they* be in good condition. Then it might be said that the fact that your watering my lawn would be good for me is not a reason for you to water my lawn; rather, it is only the fact that your watering my lawn would be good for the lawn that is a reason for you to water it.

If we accept this idea, then we have to say that the fact that your doing a thing would be good in way W is a reason for you to do it only if you want to do what would be good in way W.

[16] I thank Sarah Stroud for making this objection: she said that on this view, reasons for action "come too cheap."

Moreover, that such a fact might be a reason for you to do a thing at one time and not another. That would be the case if at the earlier time you did not want to do what would be good in way W and then came to want to do so at a later time. Perhaps some people would find this narrow construal of reasons for action attractive.

I see no theoretically important reason for rejecting this narrow construal. Or for accepting it. Whatever we wish to accomplish in moral theory can be—indeed, had better be—accomplishable whether we opt for this narrow construal of reasons for action or the broad construal of them that I have recommended.[17] I will return to this matter in Part II.

Meanwhile, I think it clear that the broad construal that I have recommended is more squarely in accord with our ideas about reasons for action. Consider a man who is standing by, watching a child drown. He has a life preserver, and could easily throw it to the child. His doing so would be good for the child. On the other hand, he cares not the least about the child, and does not want to do what would be good for it. I am inclined to think it simply false to say that there is no reason for him to throw the life preserver. There is a reason for him to do this, lying in the fact that his doing it would be good for the child. His not wanting to do what would be good for the child does not mean that there is no reason for him to do it; it means merely that he is a thoroughly bad person.

In sum, I suggest that we should reject this objection. We should agree that a fact is a reason for a person to do a thing if it

[17] The narrow construal is recommended by Bernard Williams; see his "Internal and External Reasons," which first appeared in *Rational Action*, ed. Ross Harrison (Cambridge: Cambridge University Press, 1980), and was reprinted in Bernard Williams, *Moral Luck* (Cambridge: Cambridge University Press, 1981). See also T. M. Scanlon's careful discussion of Williams's arguments in Scanlon *What We Owe to Each Other*, App. Scanlon prefers the broad construal, as do I, but I take him to agree that there is no theoretically important reason for preferring it to the narrow one.

is a fact to the effect that his doing it would be good in a way. Whether the person will do a thing there is reason for him to do, or ought to or must do it, are quite other matters, fixed by quite other considerations.

14.

Is the condition I have offered necessary as well as sufficient? One option is to say that it is, thus to say:

> (i) A fact is a reason for a person to do a thing if and only if it is a fact to the effect that his doing it would be good in a way.

Should we agree? No. It is surely plain that the fact that your *not* doing a thing would be bad in a way is a reason for you to do the thing. (The fact that your not doing the thing would be bad in a way certainly counts in favor of your doing it.) But the fact that your not doing the thing would be bad in a way is not itself a fact to the effect that your doing it would be good in a way.

Second, we should also allow that the fact that your doing a thing would be better in a way than your doing anything else is a reason for you to do the thing. (This fact too counts in favor of your doing the thing.) But this fact is not itself a fact to the effect that your doing the thing would be good in a way.

Third, we should also allow that the fact that someone has a right that you do the thing is a reason for you to do it. But this fact too is not in itself a fact to the effect that your doing the thing would be good in a way.

These facts are all evaluative, or normative, and no doubt there are other examples that could be added. I suggest that what we should say is this:

> (ii) A fact is a reason for a person to do a thing if and only if it is a fact to the effect that

his doing it would be good in a way, or

his not doing it would be bad in a way, or

his doing it would be better in a way than his doing anything
else, or

someone has a right that he do it, or . . . .

leaving room for other evaluative facts to be added.

But only other evaluative facts. For if we suppose that a reason for a person to do a thing is *itself* something that counts in favor of his doing it, then we should limit reasons for action to evaluative facts, as (ii) is intended to do. It is their being evaluative that marks these facts as reasons for action—since it is in virtue of their being evaluative that they count in favor of an action.

But perhaps we do not use the term "reason for action" as strictly as option (ii) requires? Suppose that Cora reasons to herself as follows: "My drinking some milk would increase my calcium intake, so I'll drink some."[18] And suppose that her premise is true, thus that her drinking some milk really would increase her calcium intake. Let us call that the Calcium Fact:

(The Calcium Fact) Cora's drinking some milk would increase her calcium intake.

She takes the Calcium Fact to be a reason for her to drink some milk; isn't it plausible to think that it is? If it is, then—since the Calcium Fact is not evaluative—there are facts that are reasons for action that are not evaluative, and option (ii) must be rejected.

On the other hand, there is an assumption that Cora is making, namely, that her increasing her calcium intake would be good for her. (Else she would not take the Calcium Fact to be a reason for drinking some milk.) And if that assumption is false, then the Calcium Fact is not a reason for her to drink some milk. Thus, if

[18] Notice how Cora differs from Carol of section 10, whose reasoning rested on the premise that she wanted to drink some milk.

her increasing her calcium intake would not be good for her, or would be positively bad for her, then the Calcium Fact is no reason at all for her to drink some milk.

We could say that the Calcium Fact is a reason for her to drink some milk if, but only if, her increasing her calcium intake would be good for her. If we do, we must reject the relatively simple option (ii). Alternatively, we could say that the Calcium Fact is not *itself* a reason for her to drink some milk. (It does not *itself* count in favor of her drinking some milk.) No doubt the Calcium Fact is a reason for believing that her drinking some milk would be good for her; after all, most of us really would benefit from increasing our calcium intake. We could therefore conclude that the Calcium Fact is (merely) a reason for believing that there is a reason for her to drink some milk. And we would therefore be able to retain the relatively simple option (ii).

My own impression is that nothing theoretically important turns on which of these options we choose, and I therefore recommend that we choose the relatively simple option (ii).

15.

My main concern in sections 9 through 14 has been the concept 'reason for action'. I have wished to bring out that we have an answer to the question "What is a reason for a person to do such and such?" if we help ourselves to the fact that all goodness is goodness in a way, and attend to the ways of being good.

I want to say a few things about desires by way of conclusion to Part I. I think it pays us to do so because here too it pays us to attend to the ways of being good.

We typically have a reason for wanting something, and I suggest that we should take reasons for wanting something to be similar to reasons for doing something. Thus I recommend that we say first: a fact F is a reason for a person to want a state of affairs S to obtain just in case F counts in favor of S's obtaining.

And that we say second: *F* counts in favor of *S*'s obtaining just in case *F* is a fact to the effect that *S*'s obtaining would be good in a way, or *S*'s not obtaining would be bad in a way, or . . . , where the continuation is analogous to that in (ii) of section 14.[19] If there is no such fact, then though the wanter may think there is a reason for him to want *S* to obtain, he is mistaken: there isn't.

So a person can want something and there be no reason for him to want it. Can a person want something without even believing there is a reason for him to want it? G. E. M. Anscombe invites us to imagine a man who tells us he wants a saucer of mud. "How so?" we ask. "What would be good about your getting a saucer of mud?" "Nothing," he replies; "I just happen to want to get one." Anscombe suggests that this is unintelligible, and I think she is right.[20] I think that you can't want something without thinking there is a reason for you to want it—just as (I should think) you can't expect or regret something without thinking there is a reason for you to expect or regret it.

If these ideas are right, then—even apart from the considerations I drew attention to in section 10 above—it would be no surprise if some philosophers thought that the fact that a person wants something is a reason for him to try to get it. For suppose that you want a state of affairs *S* to obtain. Suppose that you have a reason for that want, namely the fact that *S*'s obtaining would be good in a certain way *W*. A little piece of reasoning takes you from that fact to the conclusion that your trying to get *S* to obtain would also be good in way *W*; and *that* is a reason for you to try

[19] Note the availability of a more complicated condition on reasons for wanting a thing, analogous to the one available for reasons for acting; that is, one that allows for the possibility that nonevaluative facts may be reasons for wanting a thing.

[20] Anscombe, *Intention*. Warren Quinn makes a similar point in "Putting Rationality in Its Place," *Morality and Action* (Cambridge: Cambridge University Press, 1993). See also Richard Kraut, "Desire and the Human Good," *Proceedings and Addresses of the American Philosophical Association* 68, no. 2.

to get *S* to obtain. So your reason for wanting lends weight to a reason for acting, and it is therefore easy to think that the wanting is itself a reason for acting. Easy, but I suggest mistaken.

16.

I have argued in Part I that Consequentialism must be rejected on the ground that it reduces what a person ought to do to the maximizing of goodness, whereas there is no such thing as goodness. All goodness, I said, is goodness in a way. I then said that we gain more from attending to the fact that all goodness is goodness in a way than merely a refutation of Consequentialism: we are able to give an account of what it is for something to be a reason for acting.

What we should turn to now is what a person ought to do. I will not even try to produce a theory about what a person ought to do. I will only make some suggestions about the structure that I think such a theory should have.

JUDITH JARVIS THOMSON

Part Two: Advice

1.

THE WORD "ought" is probably just about as commonly used as the words "good" and "bad" are. When we say such things as "Alfred ought to drink some hot lemonade" or "Alfred ought to pay Bertha five dollars," what does or would make what we say true? These assertions have a common form, which I will write

A ought to V

—they are obtainable from that expression by replacing somebody's name for "A" and some verb or verb phrase for "V". (I should point out that what replaces "V" may be the likes of "refrain from paying Bertha" as well as the likes of "pay Bertha.") So what we are asking is: what does or would make an assertion of that form true?

It is certainly plausible to think that what a person ought to do is intimately connected with what would be good or bad. But assuming that I was right to say, as I did in Part I, that there are no such things as goodness and badness, or betterness or worseness, we cannot say

A ought to V if and only if A's V-ing would be good

or

> *A* ought to *V* if and only if *A*'s *V*-ing would be better than
> *A*'s doing any of the other things it is open to him to do.

A's *V*-ing can't be *just* good: it is at best good in this or that way
or ways. And *A*'s *V*-ing can't be *just* better than *A*'s *X*-ing, or *A*'s
Y-ing, or *A*'s *Z*-ing: it can at best be better than those in this or
that way or ways.

These considerations might tempt one to agree with those who
say that the word "ought" is at least three ways ambiguous.

On any view, the word "ought" is at least two ways ambiguous.
We say "The train ought to arrive by 3:00," and when we do, we
are not saying about the train what we say about Alfred when we
say he ought to drink some hot lemonade. What we say about the
train is roughly that the train may be expected to arrive by 3:00;
what we say about Alfred is roughly that it is advisable that he
drink some hot lemonade. I will throughout be using the word
"ought" in the latter sense, which might be called the advice
sense.

Now some people say that there is no such thing as *the* advice
sense of the word "ought": they say that "ought" has at least two
advice senses. Suppose I ask whether Alfred ought to pay Bertha
five dollars. They would reply: "What do you mean? Do you
mean 'would it be good for Alfred to pay Bertha five dollars?' If
that's what you mean, then maybe the answer is no. Or do you
mean 'would it be morally good for Alfred to pay Bertha five dollars?' If that's what you mean, then maybe the answer is yes." And
if I say "Look, what I asked was just, simply, whether Alfred ought
to pay Bertha five dollars," they reply that there is no such question—no such thing as its *just* being or not being the case that a
person ought to do a thing.

This idea might seem to square well with what I have been
saying about goodness and badness. Thus it might be said that
"ought" is multiply ambiguous: that it has a different meaning for

each way in which an act can be good. In particular, it might be said that what we need is the following:

A ought$_W$ to V if and only if A's V-ing would be better in way W than A's doing any of the other things it is open to him to do instead.

So, for example, that we should say about Alfred:

Alfred ought$_{\text{good for Alfred}}$ to pay Bertha if and only if Alfred's paying Bertha would be better for Alfred than Alfred's doing any of the other things it is open to him to do instead,

Alfred ought$_{\text{morally good}}$ to pay Bertha if and only if Alfred's paying Bertha would be morally better than Alfred's doing any of the other things it is open to him to do instead,

and no doubt also

Alfred ought$_{\text{enjoyable}}$ to pay Bertha if and only if Alfred's paying Bertha would be more enjoyable than Alfred's doing any of the other things it is open to him to do instead,

and so on for each of the ways of being good. A proponent of this idea says that if anyone asks whether Alfred ought to pay Bertha, we cannot answer the question; indeed, no question has even been asked, unless what the speaker means to be asking is, for some particular way of being good W, whether Alfred ought$_W$ to pay Bertha. We can call this the Multiple Ambiguity Idea.

It is in one way an attractive idea: as I said, it is plausible to think that what a person ought to do is intimately connected with what would be good or bad, and this idea expresses that connection in a very simple way—while accommodating the fact that all goodness is goodness in a way.

On the other hand, it is a very bad idea, and that for two reasons. First, it is wildly implausible to think that the word "ought" is multiply ambiguous in that way. Second, it gives moral goodness and badness the wrong role in assessments of what a person ought to do. I will return to moral goodness and badness later. Let us first look at the proposed ambiguity.

Suppose that Alfred is ill, and that only a dose of a certain medicine will cure him. It tastes truly awful, however. Alfred asks us "Ought I really take it?" It is a wildly implausible idea that we can reply only: "Well, your taking it would be very unpleasant, so in one sense of 'ought,' it's not the case that you ought to take it, namely the 'ought$_{enjoyable}$' sense of 'ought.' But your taking it would be good for you, so in another sense of 'ought', you ought to take it, namely the 'ought$_{goodness\ for\ Alfred}$' sense of 'ought.'" It is likely that Alfred will repeat his question: "But ought I take it?" It surely won't do to reply: "Are you deaf? I just told you that in one sense you ought to and in another sense it is not the case that you ought to, and that's all the advice that anyone can give you." We *can* give more advice: we can say what the case presumably warrants saying, namely that he ought to take the medicine.

Similarly for cases in which what is good for one is bad for another. Suppose that Alfred's paying Bertha five dollars would be good for Bertha but bad for Alfred. Alfred asks whether he ought to pay Bertha five dollars. A proponent of the Multiple Ambiguity Idea says that the only advice we are in a position to give him is that in the 'ought$_{goodness\ for\ Bertha}$' sense of "ought" Alfred ought to pay Bertha, whereas in the 'ought$_{goodness\ for\ Alfred}$' sense of "ought," it is not the case that Alfred ought to pay Bertha. Surely there remains a further question, namely whether Alfred just plain ought to pay Bertha.

In asking the question whether Alfred ought to take the medicine or ought to pay Bertha, we are using the word "ought" in *the* advice sense. That sense is what is sometimes called the 'all things considered' sense of the word. I think that "ought" has no non-all-things-considered sense.[1] But I will not argue for that here; I will merely use it in its all-things-considered sense throughout what follows.

I am going to make four suggestions that bear on it. As I said at the end of Part I, I will not offer a theory about what people ought to do. What I will do is just to draw a sketch of the structure of the theory I think we need to replace Consequentialism with. Alas, a theory with this structure would lack the simplicity of Consequentialism. But then we really shouldn't have expected a theory of what we ought to do to be simple as Consequentialists take it to be.

2.

I said it is plausible to think that what a person ought to do is intimately connected with what would be good or bad. It is very plausible to think that it is certain particular ways of being good and bad that we should be attending to.

Let us begin with the easiest cases, namely those in which what I will call (Isolation)—

> (Isolation) *A*'s *V*-ing would neither be bad for anything other than *A*, nor infringe anything's rights—

is true. They include cases in which *A*'s *V*-ing would be bad in one or more ways. Indeed, they include cases in which *A*'s *V*-ing would be bad for him. They exclude cases in which, while *A*'s *V*-ing would be bad for nothing other than *A*, it would infringe a right of *B*'s. (This is surely possible: it might be the case that *B* has a right that *A* not *V*, though it would not be bad for *B* or anything else if *A V*-ed.)

---

[1] Some philosophers think that "ought" does have a non-all-things-considered sense; I describe their view very briefly in section 8 below—see note 10.

47

The first of my four suggestions, then, is the following:

(I) If (Isolation) is true, and if also *A*'s *V*-ing would be better for him than his doing any of the other things it is open to him to do instead, then it follows that *A* ought to *V*.

I stress: I am suggesting that it *follows* that *A* ought to *V*. In particular, there is no need to add a further premise to the effect that *A* wants to do what it would be best for him to do. A person's wants do have a bearing on what he ought to do, but their bearing is indirect; we will return to the bearing of wants in the following section.

Another way to put that point is this. On some views, we should distinguish between categorical and hypothetical 'imperatives'. I put scare-quotes around the word "imperatives" since friends of those views would have us distinguish not merely between imperatives, such as "Drink that medicine" and "Pay Bertha five dollars," but also between sentences of the form that interests us, namely the likes of "Alfred ought to drink that medicine" and "Alfred ought to pay Bertha five dollars." On one interpretation of those views, then, some sentences of our form are categorical: one who asserts them asserts that the person named is to do the thing (drink the medicine, pay Bertha five dollars) whatever his wants may be. Others are hypothetical: one who asserts them asserts only that if the person wants most strongly what he would get in or by doing the thing, then he is to do it.[2] Then the point

---

[2] This is only one interpretation of the distinction between categorical and hypothetical 'imperatives'. On the interpretation I supply in the text above, the distinction is between two kinds of sentences. On another interpretation, the distinction is between two kinds of propositions a person might be asserting in asserting any given sentence of our form. Presumably there are other ways of interpreting the distinction. For our purposes, these differences do not matter.

My own view on this matter is that no such distinction can plausibly be made: that is, there is no use of the English word "ought" according to which one who asserts "*A* ought to *V*" asserts what is called a hypothetical imperative on any interpretation of that term.

I made in the preceding paragraph can now be re-put as follows: what follows from the fact (supposing it a fact) that Alfred's drinking the medicine would be best for him, and bad for nothing other than Alfred, and would infringe no one's rights, is not a hypothetical but a categorical imperative—not that he ought to drink it if he wants most strongly to do what's best for him, but, simply, that he ought to drink it.

If Alfred does not at all want to do what is best for him, then it may well be, of course, that he will not drink the medicine. So also if, while he wants to do what is best for him, he wants more strongly to avoid the medicine's nasty taste. Either way, more's the pity for him—he is behaving imprudently.

Several considerations need to be mentioned before we move on. My first suggestion was that if (Isolation) is true, and also A's V-ing would be better for him than his doing any of the other things it is open to him to do instead, then it follows that A ought to V. What if there is a tie?—that is, what if A's V-ing and A's X-ing would be equally good for him, and both better for him than his doing any of the other things it is open to him to do instead? I think that we should say here what, in Part I, I said the Consequentialist would say by way of reply to the same question. Thus we should say that in case of such a tie, it is not the case that A ought to V and not the case that A ought to X; rather, he may do either, and ought not do anything other than either.

A second consideration that needs to be mentioned is this: my first suggestion does not imply only that whether A wants to do what it would be best for him to do is irrelevant to the question

---

If I say "You ought to put antifreeze in your car in the winter," and it then turns out that you don't want to protect your car, and indeed, that it would be bad for you to protect your car, I don't say "Still, you ought to put antifreeze in your car in the winter, though of course I mean only to be asserting a hypothetical imperative." What I say is rather: "Sorry, I was mistaken in thinking you ought to put antifreeze in, etc. etc."

whether he ought to V: it implies that A's knowing, or even believing, that his V-ing would be best for him is also irrelevant to the question whether he ought to V. But that, I think, is exactly as it should be. Suppose, for example, that Alfred will be cured if and only if he drinks a certain medicine, and that his doing so would be bad for nothing other than himself, and infringe no one's rights. But suppose that while we know this, Alfred does not—suppose he not only does not know it but does not even believe it. Is it true, all the same, that he ought to drink the medicine? I recommend that we say that it is true. For suppose he asks us whether he ought to drink it. It would be weird to reply that we can't tell whether he ought to drink the medicine until he first tells us what he believes about it and about himself. We don't need to find out what he believes: whatever his beliefs may be, he ought to drink it. He has asked us for advice, and that is the advice we should give him.

Similarly, my first suggestion implies that what A would be intending in V-ing (if he V-ed) is also irrelevant to the question whether he ought to V. That too is as it should be. If Alfred asks us whether he ought to drink the medicine, it would be equally weird to reply that we can't tell until he first tells us what he would be intending in drinking it. Whatever he intends, he ought to drink that medicine.

I think it clear quite generally that what fixes whether a person ought to do a thing is not the person's subjective state of mind, but instead the objective facts of the situation he is in. I will summarize this point by saying that the question what a person ought to do is (not subjective, but rather) objective.[3]

There is a third consideration that needs to be mentioned. I said that we were to be considering cases in which

[3] For more on this point, see Jonathan Bennett's distinction between first-order and second-order morality in his *The Act Itself* (Oxford: Oxford University Press, 1995).

(Isolation) *A*'s *V*-ing would neither be bad for anything other than *A*, nor infringe anything's rights

is true. Why "not be bad for anything other than *A*" rather than "not be bad for any person other than *A*"? I meant to be setting aside cases in which *A*'s *V*-ing would be bad for anything. An animal, for example. Or for a living thing of some other kind, such as a plant. Or for some nonliving thing, such as an artifact or a river. There obviously is such a thing as an act's being bad for an animal or a plant; if less obvious, it is also true that an act may be bad for an artifact or a river. Wherever *A*'s *V*-ing would be bad for something other than *A*, then that is in one or another way relevant to whether he ought, or even may, *V*: the question whether *A* ought to *V* is not settled by the mere fact that it would be best for him to do the thing and bad for no other person.

Again, why "not infringe anything's rights" rather than "not infringe any person's rights"? I meant to leave open that things other than people have rights. Organizations. Animals, perhaps. Wherever *A*'s *V*-ing would infringe anything's rights, then that is in one or another way relevant to whether he ought, or even may, *V*: the question whether *A* ought to *V* is not settled by the mere fact that it would be best for him to do the thing and infringe no person's rights.

We will turn to cases in which (Isolation) is not true in section 5.

3.

It is intuitively clear that the concepts 'good for' and 'bad for' play an important role in fixing whether a person ought to do a thing. We should therefore have a look at them.

There is a large literature on what it is for something to be good for a person, but I think that any plausible theory will serve our purposes well enough.

51

I assume three constraints on the plausibility of a theory about what it is for something to be good for a person. First, the theory must allow for the possibility that a person's doing a thing would be good for him, even best for him of all his alternatives, and yet bad for another person. Similarly, it must allow for the possibility that a person's doing a thing would be bad for him, even worst of all his alternatives, and yet good for another person. That this is a constraint on the plausibility of a theory is probably obvious enough.

A second constraint is stronger: the theory must allow for the possibility that a person's doing a thing would be good for him, even best for him of all his alternatives, though he ought not do it; and that his doing a thing would be bad for him, even worst for him of all his alternatives, though he ought to do it. Perhaps this second constraint is also obvious.

But even if it is obvious, it does have a certain bite, for there are views according to which it is mistaken: on those views, it can't be, can't *really* be, can't really be *in the long run* or *all things considered* good for a person to do what he ought not, or bad for him to do what he ought to do. Friends of these ideas think that moral requirement in particular has this feature. On their view, the nature of a person, and the content of moral requirement, are such that necessarily, a person's obedience to the requirement conduces to the good of the person. This strikes me as an excessively high-minded conception of the nature of a person, and therefore of what is good for a person; I will not argue against it, but merely set it aside.

The third constraint is this: the theory must allow for the possibility that a person's doing a thing would not be good for him, even though it is what he most wants to do—and indeed, even if his wants are appropriately restricted.

What I have in mind here is this. There is something right about the idea that what is good for a person is importantly con-

nected with satisfaction of his wants. If a man most wants to become a veterinarian, what could possibly make it fail to be good
for him to do so? No doubt he'd make more money as a lawyer,
but that hardly matters. If a woman most wants to spend her free
time knitting scarves for her friends, what could possibly make it
fail to be good for her to do so? On some views, then, what is
good for a person is not just importantly connected with satisfaction of his wants, but analyzable into satisfaction of wants—thus:
what is good for a person is what conduces to satisfaction of his
wants.

But no one thinks this idea even remotely plausible unless the
wants that matter to goodness for a person are appropriately restricted. The relevant wants are not passing wants, as where a
person has a momentary desire to kick somebody in the shin. Nor
wants due to ignorance, as where a person wants to drink a certain
liquid, not knowing that it contains cyanide. Nor wants due to
improper preference-bending, as where a person has been hyp-
notized. The relevant wants are, rather, relatively stable, resting
on correct information, and autonomously arrived at. Another
way to put the point is this: the relevant wants are those a person
would have "in a cool hour," in possession of full relevant information, and under no improper pressure to conform his will to
that of others. These are vague conditions, but it is an intuitively
attractive idea that assessing what would be good for a person
does require assessing exactly these things, hard though it may be
to arrive at a correct judgment about them.

Analogously for badness for a person: what is bad for a person
is what interferes with satisfaction of his relevant wants.[4]

---

[4] This account of goodness and badness for a person is complicated. I think it pays to
draw attention to the fact that there is no future in the idea that goodness for a person is
analyzable, more simply, in terms of needs. A person needs food and drink, and it is good
for the person to get these things. But your doing a thing might be good for you without
its being the case that you *need* it done. For example, it might well be good for you to learn
Russian without its being the case that you need to learn Russian. What a person needs is

Now the third constraint I impose on a theory of goodness for people rules this attractive idea out, so it has even more bite than the second constraint. My reason for thinking the idea should be ruled out is this. Consider a doctor who leaves her comfortable practice to go across country to help deal with an epidemic at risk of her own health, perhaps even of her life. Going across country to do this is what she most wants to do, and we can suppose that her wants meet the restrictions I mentioned; are we to say that her doing so is good for her? Or again, consider a man who gives a kidney to his friend, who needs it for life, despite the risk to his health of doing so. Giving the kidney is what he most wants to do, and we can suppose that his wants too meet the restrictions I mentioned; are we to say here that his doing so is good for him? Surely it is intuitively wrong to say that these acts are good for their agents. And we make too little of the moral impressiveness of what they do if we say that what they do is good for them. Their acts are morally impressive precisely because, though good for others, they are not good for them.

The possibility I point to here is not restricted to cases in which an act is morally impressive. Consider a master chess player who spends his time studying chess, gets no exercise, and smokes heavily because he finds that smoking helps him to concentrate. These are things he wants to do because he wants to become world champion. But I think we cannot at all plausibly say that doing them is good for him.[5]

---

not just anything that it would be good for him to get, but rather what it would be bad for him to not get. And I see no more reason to think (indeed, less reason to think) that badness for a person is analyzable in terms of needs than there is to think that needs are analyzable in terms of badness-for.

So also for animals, plants, and artifacts. Animals and plants also need food and drink, and it is good for them to get these things. A lawn mower may need oiling; if so, it would be good for it to get oiled. But the fact that animals, plants, and artifacts need these things is a product of its being bad for them to not get them.

[5] This is obvious enough if his efforts do not succeed, so that he does not become

What works against the idea that what is good for a person is what conduces to satisfaction of his wants is the idea that what is good for a person is what conduces to his health. Many people do sometimes want most to do what interferes with their health, and this even though their wants do meet the restrictions I mentioned above.

So perhaps we should instead opt for a theory according to which goodness for people is analyzable into conduciveness to health? There are at least two objections to this idea. First, the idea is far too narrow. It might be good for your daughter to be accepted by a good law school; I find it hard to believe that this would conduce to her health. Second, and more interesting, if we ask why it is good for a person to be healthy, there seems to be an answer: health does of course have its special pleasures, but what seems fundamental to its value to us is that it is a prerequisite for our being able to do much of what most people most deeply want to do. These two objections head us back toward the idea that goodness for people consists in satisfaction of wants.

My own impression is that the best theory of what is good for a person lies somewhere in between these two ideas. If this is right, then it is clear that, if not exactly how, a person's wants are relevant to what he ought to do: they are so by being relevant to what it would be good for him to do.

Fortunately for our purposes, it does not really matter exactly where, between those two ideas, the best theory of what is good for a person lies. Our main concern will be what is to be said of cases in which a person's doing a thing would be good (or bad) for

---

champion. But what if they do and he therefore does? Should we say (i) that his becoming champion is good for him, though his taking the necessary means to that end was not? Or (ii) that, given those were the necessary means to that end, and that they were not good for him, it follows that his becoming champion is not itself good for him? or (iii) that, given his becoming champion is good for him, it follows that his taking those means was, after all, good for him? I leave this open.

him, but bad (or good) for another person. So long as the criteria for goodness for and badness for a person are general, in the sense that they bear on both parties—and so long as the three constraints I listed are met—that will suit us well enough.

4.

Less has been written about what is good or bad for an animal or plant, and hardly anything about what is good or bad for an artifact or a river. I will have to be brief about these matters.[6]

What is good for a plant is obviously what conduces to its health. I said there were two objections to the idea that goodness for people is analyzable into conduciveness to health; neither arises in the case of plants. First, everything that is good for a plant, whatever it may be, conduces to its health: more strongly, if something is good for a plant, then that is because and only because it conduces to the plant's health. Second, if we ask why it is good for a plant to be healthy, there is no answer. Plants have no wants, and a fortiori, their being healthy is not good for them because it is a prerequisite for their being able to do what they want.

This difference between what is good for people and what is good for plants is pretty plainly due to the very fact that people have wants and plants do not.

Even the higher animals are more like plants in this respect than they are like people. Unlike plants, they do have wants; unlike people, their range of wants is narrow. (No doubt that is due to the fact that their range of experiences is narrow. They have a more or less wide variety of sensory experiences, and they feel pleasure and pain; but they feel no resentment, indignation, am-

---

[6] My own views about these matters appear, in greater detail, in "The Right and the Good," *Journal of Philosophy* 94, no. 6. Though I still think that my remarks there about goodness for other things are true, my remarks there about goodness for people now strike me as false—they are argued against in section 3 above.

bition, pride, envy, admiration, and so on.) In light of the fact that they are conscious beings, a plausible account of what is good for them should presumably lie somewhere between that for people and that for plants.

What is it for a person, animal, or plant to be healthy? Curiously enough, I think we are helped if we have a look at artifacts first.

Your doing a thing might be good for your lawn mower—for example, oiling it might be good for it. How so? Oiling it would conduce to its being in good condition. What does that come to? Oiling it would conduce to its being able to do what it was designed by its manufacturer to do, namely enable a person who uses it properly to mow lawns easily, safely, and well. We don't call an artifact that is in good condition a healthy artifact, but the idea is surely similar.

Similar in that a living creature is healthy just in case it is able to do what it was 'designed by nature' to do—among other things, grow in ways suitable to members of its species, and propagate itself. Animals are designed by nature to do more than plants are, and human beings to do more things still. But feeding any living creature the food suitable to members of its species, and in a suitable amount, would be good for it in that doing so would conduce to its being in a condition in which it is able to do those things.

It is important to recognize that what is good for an animal or plant is not reducible to what is good for people. It might be good for a cat's owner to have it declawed; it is nevertheless not good for the cat to do so. It might be good for a lawn's owner to kill the dandelions that grow in it; it is not good for the dandelions to do so. What is good for human beings plays a more subtle role in the case of artifacts. There are such things as artifacts because of human wants. But whether or not doing a thing is good for an artifact is not a function of human wants. I might want my lawn mower to become unusable to mow lawns with; that is compatible with its being bad for the lawn mower to do so. So also, I should think, for animals and plants that are not in fact designed by nature but instead by human beings—that is, animals and plants that are bred by humans for special purposes: once bred, what is good for them is a function of their design and not our purposes.

Rivers, lakes, mountains, and ravines are quite another matter. In their case, it is what is good for human beings that fixes what is good for them. The Charles River in Massachusetts had become polluted; it was good for the river that measures be taken to decrease the pollution. But that was not because doing so conduced to the river's being able to do what rivers are designed by nature to do: there is no such thing. Rather it was because human beings wished to be able to sail, fish, and swim in the river, and to avoid the nasty look and smell that pollution brings with it.

These differences must surely have a bearing on whether a person ought or ought not or may do a thing where the person's doing it would be best for him but bad for a thing of one or another of these kinds. A theory about what a person ought to do should deal with them. I have no such theory, however, and will only be able to indicate the structure into which I suggest they should be fitted.

5.

What we have been looking at so far are the easy cases, namely those in which

(Isolation) A's V-ing would neither be bad for anything other than A nor infringe anything's rights

is true. The first of my four suggestions was about those easy cases, and it said:

(I) If (Isolation) is true, and if also *A*'s *V*-ing would be better
for him than his doing any of the other things it is open
to him to do instead, then it follows that *A* ought to *V*.

We should turn now to the hard cases, namely those in which
(Isolation) is false. They are the ones of most concern to moral
philosophy.

The second of my four suggestions is this:

(II) Justice and generosity are second-order ways of being
good; injustice and (what I will call) miserliness are second-order ways of being bad.

For a reason that will emerge in section 7, it is injustice and
miserliness that will primarily matter to us. So let us begin with
injustice.

To act unjustly is to fail to do what is owed; that is, it is to fail
to do what another person has a right to one's doing. More precisely, to act unjustly is to fail to do what another person has a
non-overridden right to one's doing. Suppose that Alfred has
a right that you meet him at the corner of High and Main at
3:00 P.M. today. How might Alfred have acquired that right? Perhaps you promised him that you would meet him there then.
Here are two kinds of case in which Alfred's right is overridden.
(i) Bertha has a more stringent right that you not meet Alfred
there then. Perhaps you promised her that you would not do so,
which is what gave her a right that you not do so. What would
mark her right as more stringent? Well, perhaps while Alfred will
merely be annoyed if you do not turn up on time, she will suffer
greatly if you do. (ii) Alfred's right that you meet him there then
is weak (that is, nonstringent), and no one has a right that you not
be there then, but your being there then would be very bad for
you, or for Bertha, or for Bertha and Charles. Perhaps while Alfred will (once again) merely be annoyed if you do not turn up on
time, you or Bertha or both Bertha and Charles will suffer greatly

59

if you do. In cases of kinds (i) and (ii), Alfred's right that you meet him at the corner of High and Main at 3:00 P.M. today is over-ridden; and if you fail to meet him there then, your doing so is not unjust.[7]

By hypothesis, Alfred has a right that you meet him at the cor-ner of High and Main at 3:00 P.M. today. What if (iii) Bertha has an equally stringent right that you not meet him there then? (For simplicity, let us suppose that no one else would be affected, whichever you do.) Here we have a tie again. I think that nothing theoretically interesting turns on which choice we make; since I think it simpler, and somewhat more plausible, to conclude that neither of them has a non-overridden right in respect of your meeting or not meeting Alfred, I will assume so. (A good idea for you in such a situation would be to try to get them to agree to your flipping a coin. If they do, then presumably the winner, and only the winner, has a non-overridden right.)

In sum, then: to act unjustly is to fail to do what something has a non-overridden right to one's doing.

A feature of this account of acting unjustly calls for explicit mention. What I refer to is the fact that according to this account, the question whether a person's act is unjust does not turn on

[7] Some philosophers hold the view that there is no such thing as a right that is over-ridden; on their view, all rights are 'absolute'. Thus they would say that in cases of kinds (i) and (ii), Alfred has no right that you be there then, for the facts about Bertha in (i) and about you or Bertha or Bertha and Charles in (ii) make Alfred cease to have the right you gave him when you made your promise to him. Other philosophers—I include myself—hold the view that Alfred does have the right you gave him, though it is overridden, and justice therefore does not require your according it to him. My reason for preferring this second view is the fact that if you do not keep your promise to Alfred, you will at a minimum owe him an apology: this fact seems to me to show that the right you gave him did not simply go out of existence. I will throughout assume without argument that this second view is correct. For our purposes, it does not really matter which is correct, and what I say below could easily enough be revised in such a way as to square with the first view.

I supply more detail on these matters in *The Realm of Rights* (Cambridge: Harvard University Press, 1990).

what the person's beliefs or intentions are. What fixes whether the person's act is unjust is not the person's subjective state of mind, but instead the objective fact that something else does or does not have a non-overridden right against him. That seems to me exactly as it should be. Suppose Alfred does not believe that anything has a non-overridden right that he send Bertha a check for fifty dollars. But suppose that is because he has simply forgotten that he had promised her that he would, and suppose also that her right that he do so is non-overridden. Then his failing to send her a check would be unjust. If it is not his fault that he forgot his promise, then we may well think he would not be to blame for failing to send her a check; but that his failure would be unjust seems quite clear. I will summarize this point by saying that the question whether a person's act is unjust is objective—just as, as I said earlier, the question whether a person ought to do a thing is objective. I think it clear that this is true of justice too.[8]

Let us turn now to miserliness. I will so use that word that it stands for the contrary of generosity. My use of the word is therefore broader than the ordinary use of it, for I think that we call an act miserly only where its agent is mean or grudging about money. Suppose that Bertha is drowning and Alfred alone can save her, as it might be, by throwing her his life preserver. If Alfred refuses to do this on the ground that he is feeling tired, and does not want to bother, then I will say that his refusal to throw it is miserly, despite the fact that his refusal is not due to meanness about money.

By way of preliminary characterization, I will describe as "miserly" any act that provides its agent with a small gain—whether

---

[8] It might pay to make explicit that my point in the text has to do with *acts* only. The questions whether a *person* is unjust and whether a person is just are not, or anyway are not wholly, objective. I will shortly opt for a similar point about the questions whether an act is miserly, and whether an act is generous; opting for it is compatible with accepting that the questions whether a person is miserly, and whether a person is generous, are not, or anyway are not wholly, objective.

financial or otherwise—or even no gain at all, despite the act's being very bad for another person. Thus an act of gratuitous cruelty, inconsiderateness, or discourtesy may also be miserly.

Why "another person"? Is it only where the 'victim' of the act is a person that an act is miserly? I will suppose not. If animals lack rights, then it is not possible for one's treatment of them to be unjust; I mean to allow that it is possible for one's treatment of an animal to be miserly whether or not animals have rights. This use of "miserly" is as it should be if miserliness is to be the contrary of generosity, for I should think it possible to be generous to an animal.

What about plants, artifacts, and rivers? Rivers we can set aside, since nothing is bad for them except by way of being bad for people. I am inclined to think, however, that we should allow for the possibility that one's treatment of a plant or artifact is miserly. If you gain nothing from destroying a tree or a painting, by which I mean to include that it would cost you nothing to refrain from destroying it, then I will say that your treatment of it is miserly—even if there is no person whose property rights you violate, or whom you affect for the worse.

So here is an interesting difference between injustice and miserliness: your treatment of a thing can be unjust only if the thing is a right-holder, whereas your treatment of a thing can be miserly even if it is not. I will draw attention to yet another difference between injustice and miserliness shortly.

In any case, let us emend the preliminary characterization of miserliness that I gave above. It is surely right to think that Alfred's *V*-ing is miserly only if

(i) Alfred's *V*-ing provides Alfred with at most a small gain, despite its being very bad for something else

is true.

Another condition is necessary, however. Suppose that (i) is true of Alfred's *V*-ing. Suppose, however, that someone has a non-overridden right to Alfred's *V*-ing. Then I will say that Alfred's *V*-ing is not miserly.

Here is an example. Suppose that Bertha is using Alfred's typewriter without his permission; she needs it to complete some work she is doing, the doing of which is important to her. Suppose that Alfred has no need of the typewriter himself, and indeed, that he would gain nothing at all by requesting its return. Suppose he nevertheless requests its return. Then his requesting its return gains him nothing, despite being very bad for Bertha. It sounds, therefore, as if Alfred's requesting the return of the typewriter is miserly. But suppose, last, that Cora has a non-overridden right that Alfred request the return of the typewriter. (Alfred has promised Cora that he will get it back from Bertha to give to Cora, who needs it more than Bertha does.) Now it is clear that Alfred's requesting the return of the typewriter is not miserly.

So we need to add a further condition on miserliness: Alfred's *V*-ing is miserly only if

(ii) Nobody has a non-overridden right that Alfred *V*

is also true.

Condition (ii) is not unique to miserliness, for it holds of generosity too. If somebody has a non-overridden right that Alfred *V*, then his *V*-ing is not miserly. So similarly: if somebody has a non-overridden right that Alfred *V*, then his *V*-ing is not generous. (It is not generous in a person to pay his grocer's bill on time, however good for his grocer his doing so would be.)

In sum, I take it that conditions (i) and (ii) are both necessary for an act to be miserly. Are they jointly sufficient? I should think not. That is because of a feature of miserliness—and generosity—that I will call context-dependence.

Suppose that I have never given to the needy, and it is proposed to me now that I make a small contribution to them. If I refuse, my refusing is miserly; indeed, it is very miserly. By contrast, suppose that you have very often given to the needy, and it is proposed to you now that you make yet another small contribution to them. If you refuse, your refusal is markedly less miserly, and perhaps is not miserly at all. (Why so? Presumably because your total contribution is already not small.) This feature of miserliness is what I am calling context-dependence.

Context-dependence is also a feature of generosity: your making a further small contribution now is the more generous given you have very often contributed in the past.

But context-dependence is not a feature of either injustice or justice, and therefore constitutes yet another difference between injustice and miserliness. My failing to pay my grocer's bill on time is not less unjust if I have very often paid my grocer's bill on time in the past. Nor is my paying my grocer's bill on time more just if I have paid it on time very often in the past.[9]

Expressing the context-dependence of miserliness in the form of a further condition on miserliness would be a complex business, and not, I think, an interesting one. So I leave open how this is to be done. I leave open also the possibility that further conditions should be placed on miserliness.

But what I do not leave open is the possibility of adding a condition concerning the agent's subjective state of mind. I will so use the word "miserly" that the answer to the question whether a person's act is or is not miserly does not turn on his beliefs or intentions: rather it turns on what he (objectively) does, as con-

[9] I will suggest in section 7 below that we ought to avoid miserliness and injustice. Taking liberties with Kant's terminology, we might say that we have perfect duties to avoid miserliness and injustice in the sense that we are on all occasions to avoid both—but that we also have an imperfect duty to avoid miserliness in the sense that miserliness (unlike injustice) is context-dependent.

dition (i) requires, and on whether nobody has a non-overridden right against him, as condition (ii) requires. I will summarize this point by saying that the question whether an act is miserly is objective. Miserliness, however, was to be the contrary of generosity; and isn't our ordinary use of "generous" subjective? I think it is, or that it at least mostly is. Suppose that muddled Alfred intends to be helping Bertha, and believes that he is succeeding in doing so, but he is mistaken: what he is doing in fact harms her. Do we say that his act was nevertheless generous? I think we do.

On the other hand, I am not sure that our use of "generous" is always subjective in this way. Consider the muddled miser, who intends not to help, and thinks he is not helping. Unbeknownst to him, however, he is in fact helping. Mightn't we say that unbeknownst to him, his act was generous? (If a person says "I didn't mean to be generous," do we always conclude that his act was not generous? Mightn't we sometimes reply "All the same, you were"?)

In any case, I will throughout use the word "generous" in such a way that it—like its intended contrary, "miserly"—is objective. The muddled miser, whose act was (as I will say) generous certainly deserves no praise for it; he may even deserve blame for it. By contrast, while muddled Alfred's act was (as I will say) not generous, and perhaps was even miserly, he may deserve no blame for it; he may even deserve praise for it.

6.

To return now to my suggestions. The second of my four suggestions was:

(II) Justice and generosity are second-order ways of being good; injustice and (what I will call) miserliness are second-order ways of being bad.

65

We now have in hand an account of injustice and anyway a good enough preliminary account of miserliness to be able to see, as follows, that (II) is true.

It is presumably clear enough that injustice and miserliness are ways of being bad, and justice and generosity are ways of being good.

My ground for saying that injustice is a second-order way of being bad has already emerged, for what I have in mind about it is this. The answer to the question whether an act is unjust turns in part on whether those affected by it have the relevant rights; but it also turns in part on whether those rights are overridden, and that turns in part on how good or bad the act would be for those affected by it. Goodness-for and badness-for are first-order ways of being good; whether an act is unjust cannot be settled unless it is first settled how good or bad it would be in the relevant first-order ways.

That miserliness is a second-order way of being bad is perhaps even clearer than that injustice is—for it is clear that whether an act is miserly is in part a function of how good refraining would have been for others, and how bad refraining would have been for the agent.

The analogue of this point also holds of justice and generosity.

A word or two should probably be said here about moral goodness and badness. I said that injustice and miserliness are ways of being bad, and justice and generosity are ways of being good. Couldn't we have said that the first pair are ways of being morally bad, and the second pair ways of being morally good?

I am inclined to think that the ordinary use of the terms "morally good" and "morally bad" is such that the questions whether they apply to an act are subjective, not objective. Thus consider again a person who means to be acting justly, and thinks he is succeeding in doing so. As I said, he may be mistaken: it may be that his act is in fact unjust. If the mistake is not his fault, then (as I said) we may well think he is not to blame for his unjust act. Indeed, he might even deserve praise for it. Suppose he does deserve praise for it. Then I think we would conclude that, although his act was unjust, it was morally good.

Similarly, consider again the muddled miser, who intends not to help, and thinks he is not helping. Unbeknownst to him, however, he is in fact helping. I said I would so use the word "generous" that his act is generous. He does not of course deserve praise for it; rather, he may deserve blame for it. Suppose he does deserve blame for it. Then I think we would conclude that, although his act was generous, it was morally bad.

In short, our ordinary use of those terms seems to me to be such that their applicability to an act turns on its agent's subjective state of mind, in particular, on his beliefs and intentions.

I see no good reason to reject that usage, and I therefore think we should agree that the questions whether an act is morally good or morally bad cut across the questions whether it is just or unjust, generous or miserly.

Moreover, we should agree that the questions whether an act is morally good or morally bad cuts across the questions whether its agent ought or ought not be doing what he is doing—for, as I argued earlier, the questions whether a person ought to do a thing, or ought not do it, are not subjective, but instead objective.

Our concern here is what a person ought or ought not do. I therefore bypass moral goodness and badness.

7.

The third of my four suggestions is about what a person ought to do:

(III) *A* ought to *V* if his not *V*-ing would be either unjust or miserly, and *A* ought not *V* if his *V*-ing would be either unjust or miserly.

I think that, given the characterizations of injustice and miserliness I offered in section 5, this suggestion is intuitively very plausible.

We should notice that (III) says "if," and not "if and only if." That is because there may well be other grounds for saying that a person ought to do a thing or ought not do it than injustice and miserliness. For example, my first suggestion said:

(I) If (Isolation) is true, and if also *A*'s *V*-ing would be better for him than his doing any of the other things it is open to him to do instead, then it follows that *A* ought to *V*—

where (Isolation) says:

(Isolation) *A*'s *V*-ing would neither be bad for anything other than *A*, nor infringe anything's rights.

Wherever (Isolation) is true, *A*'s *V*-ing is neither unjust nor miserly; yet it may all the same be the case that *A* ought to *V*, or ought to refrain from *V*-ing. And we should not suppose that the word "ought" has different senses, according as injustice and miserliness are or are not in question. I have invited you to agree that there is such a thing as *the* advice sense of the word "ought," which is the sense that I am taking it to have throughout.

It is worth noticing that, given (III),

(II) Justice and generosity are second-order ways of being good; injustice and (what I will call) miserliness are second-order ways of being bad

is more important than it may initially have appeared. Suppose that Alfred's doing a thing would be good for him, but that his doing it would be unjust. If (III) is true, then Alfred ought not do the thing. That, I am sure, will seem plausible to most people. Perhaps not to others. But whether it seems plausible or not,

many people ask for a justification. *Why* does the fact that Alfred's
doing the thing would be unjust yield that he ought not do it?—
when, by hypothesis, it would be good for him to do it?

Another way to put this question is this. I said in Part I that the
fact that a person's doing a thing would be good in a way counts
in favor of his doing it, and the fact that a person's doing a thing
would be bad in a way counts against his doing it. For (III) to be
true, it is required that the fact that Alfred's doing a thing would
be unjust (hence bad in a way) counts more strongly against his
doing it than the fact that his doing it would be good for him
counts in favor of his doing it. Why (it is asked) should we think
this true?

If (II) is true, this question has not the interest it has been
thought to have. According to (II), we are not to weigh the fact
that Alfred's doing the thing would be good for him against the
fact that his doing it would be unjust, leaving open the possibility
that the fact that his doing it would be good for him counts more
strongly in favor of his doing it. For given that injustice is a second-order way of being bad, the fact that his doing the thing
would be good for him has *already* been taken into consideration
in arriving at the conclusion that his doing it would be unjust. To
allow the fact that his doing the thing would be good for him to
have a further, independent, bearing on what he ought to do
would be to double-count it.

There is a more general point in the offing. Suppose that Alfred's doing a thing would be unjust or miserly. According to
(III), it follows that Alfred ought not do it. In saying that Alfred
ought not do it, I am saying that Alfred ought not do it, whatever
the consequences of his doing it—that is, however good the consequences of his doing it may be in whatever ways they may be
good. That his act would possess the second-order features of
being unjust or miserly is a conclusion arrivable at only after

consideration of the first-order ways in which Alfred's doing the thing would be good.

Suggestions (I), (II), and (III) can be connected in the following way: we can say that they jointly yield that what a person ought to do is what gives adequate weight to the interests of all who would be affected. Suppose that (Isolation) is true of Alfred's drinking some hot lemonade. It follows that only Alfred's own interests are relevant to the question whether he ought to drink some. According to (I), he ought to drink some if his doing so is best for him. And we can say: his doing so would give adequate weight to his own interests. His choosing any option less good for him would give inadequate weight to his own interests—it would be imprudent.

Suppose, however, that (Isolation) is not true of Alfred's drinking some hot lemonade. (Perhaps he has promised Bertha that he would not.) Then the interests of others are relevant to the question whether he ought to drink some. According to (III), he ought not drink some if his doing so would be unjust or miserly; according to (II), the question whether it would be turns in part on how good or bad his doing so would be for him and for those others. If his doing so would be unjust or miserly, so that he ought not, then we can say: his doing so would be his failing to give adequate weight to the interests of all who would be affected—those of the others as well as his own.

8.

But is

(III) *A* ought to *V* if his not *V*-ing would be either unjust or miserly, and *A* ought not *V* if his *V*-ing would be either unjust or miserly

true? There is a possible objection to it that I think worth taking note of.

Suppose that A's V-ing would be unjust. According to (III), it follows that A ought not V. Can we consistently also suppose that his not V-ing would be miserly? Suppose we can. Let us do so, then: we now suppose also that A's not V-ing would be miserly. According to (III), it follows that he ought to V. So it follows both that A ought not V, and also that A ought to V.

Some philosophers are quite content to make room for the possibility that

(1) A ought not V

and

(2) A ought to V

are both true.[10]

Other philosophers—I include myself—think it is not possible that (1) and (2) are both true. We must therefore either reject (III) or rebut the objection to it that I have just drawn attention to.

The rebuttal is easy, however, given my characterizations of injustice and miserliness. I said just above: suppose that A's V-ing would be unjust. I then asked: can we consistently also suppose that his not V-ing would be miserly? The answer is that we can't. Given my characterization of injustice, A's V-ing is unjust only if

(3) Somebody has a non-overridden right that A not V

---

[10] It is obviously not possible that (2) and

(*) It is not the case that A ought to V

are both true, so that if (1) entails (*), then those philosophers are mistaken—that is, it is not possible that (1) and (2) are both true. But those philosophers simply deny that (1) entails (*).

The philosophers I refer to here are those who accept that there are what they call "moral dilemmas." I indicated earlier that my own use of "ought" would be all-things-considered, and it is surely clear that if "ought" is construed as I construe it, then (1) does entail (*), and (1) is therefore incompatible with (2).

is true. But given my characterization of miserliness, A's not V-ing is miserly only if

(4) Nobody has a non-overridden right that A not V

is true. It is plain that (3) and (4) are incompatible. So it cannot be the case both that Alfred's V-ing is unjust and that his not V-ing is miserly.

9.

My fourth suggestion emerges on consideration of the question why I have focused on injustice and miserliness, which are ways of being bad, rather than on justice and generosity, which are ways of being good.

To begin with justice. According to (III), the fact that A's V-ing would be unjust entails that A ought not V. But the fact that A's V-ing would be just does not entail that A ought to V. That, I should think, is obvious. There might well be cases in which you have several options for action—as it might be, several ways of distributing a benefit you owe—each entirely just, there being no one of them that you ought to choose.

A similar point holds of generosity. It might well be that while you cannot give aid to both Alfred and Bertha, giving aid to Alfred and giving aid to Bertha would each be generous, neither option being such that you ought to choose it.

In short, we cannot say that a person ought to do a thing if his doing of it would be either just or generous.

A further, and more interesting, reason why we cannot say that a person ought to do a thing if his doing of it would be either just or generous issues from a fact about generosity. An act can be more or less generous, and a very generous act may be, as it is sometimes put, supererogatory, that is, as we say, 'above and beyond the call of duty'. The person who saved a life at risk of his own acted very generously. It does not follow that he did what he ought. Indeed, it would not have been true to say of him that he ought to save that life. What he did for the other person was beyond what he ought.

This point does not also hold of justice. While some generous acts are beyond what one ought, no just act is. No matter, for our purposes. The fact remains that we cannot say that a person ought to do a thing if his doing of it would be either just *or* generous.

I said earlier that what a person ought to do is what gives adequate weight to the interests of all affected—not lavish weight. What "You ought" requires of us is the adequate minimum. That is my fourth suggestion:

(IV) Doing what one ought only requires giving the adequate minimum weight to the interests of all who are affected.

It pays to stress, however, that accepting (IV) does not commit us to a conclusion about praise. Certainly the person who saved a life at risk of his own deserves much praise for doing so: and I should think, by contrast, that one rarely deserves praise for doing what one ought. But it may on occasion be the case that a person does deserve praise for doing what he ought—as, for example, where his avoiding injustice requires more courage and a stronger will than are normally required in our dealings with others.

Suggestion (IV) says *all* who are affected, which of course includes A himself. On the one hand, whether someone's right against A is non-overridden turns on what is good or bad for A as well as on what is good or bad for others. On the other hand, there are limits to what avoiding miserliness requires of us. I said that the person who saved a life at risk of his own acted very generously, and deserves much praise for doing so. Would it be very generous, deserving of much praise, to cure someone's sore throat at risk of one's life? I hardly think so. The beneficiary's gain is too small in comparison with the loss the agent risks. There is nothing praiseworthy in making a major sacrifice in order to forestall another person's small loss. Surely such an act is not merely not praiseworthy, its agent ought not perform it. Why so? Presumably the answer lies in the fact that a person who makes a major sacrifice in order to forestall another person's small loss does not give adequate weight to his own interests— and a fortiori does not give adequate weight to the interests of all who are affected.

10.

It is time now to make contact with the proposals I made in Part I about reasons for action. I said there that the concept 'reason for a person to do such and such' has been thought to have an intimate connection with the concept 'ought'. Some philosophers hold that A ought to V only if there is a reason for A to V. Or even more strongly: A ought to V if and only if V-ing is precisely what there is most reason for A to do.

I then proposed that a fact is a reason for A to V if and only if it is a fact to the effect that

A's V-ing would be good in a way, or
A's not V-ing would be bad in a way, or
A's V-ing would be better in a way than A's doing anything else, or
Someone has a right that A V, or . . . ,

leaving open that other evaluative facts should be added to this list.

What has emerged in the preceding sections is the idea that some of these kinds of fact are good reason to believe that A ought to V. Indeed, some are themselves conclusive reasons to believe that A ought to V. Thus the fact that A's not V-ing would be unjust, or would be miserly, is conclusive reason to believe that A

ought to V. And some are—not themselves, but in conjunction with other facts—conclusive reasons to believe that A ought to V. Thus the fact that A's V-ing would be better for him than his doing anything else is not itself conclusive reason to believe A ought to V, but the conjunction of it with (Isolation) is.

Suppose we say that wherever there is a fact that is—or is, in conjunction with (Isolation)—conclusive reason to believe that A ought to V, then there is "most reason" for A to V. Then we can say: A ought to V if V-ing is what there is most reason for A to do.

Can we also say: A ought to V *only if* V-ing is what there is most reason for A to do? I should think it very plausible that we can. That a person ought to do a thing is not a fact that floats free of anything that might be thought to make it a fact; and what would make it a fact is surely facts of the kinds we have been looking at. Have we have looked at all the relevant kinds? An agent's advantage, where (Isolation) is true, covers a good bit of territory. So does injustice. So does miserliness, understood in the way I have been taking it. (As I said, an act of gratuitous cruelty, inconsiderateness, or discourtesy may be miserly.) But I will not try to argue that there are no others.

In any case, if the stronger claim—namely that A ought to V *if and only if* V-ing is what there is most reason for A to do—is true, then so also is the weaker claim that A ought to V only if there is reason for A to V.

However, the availability of these conclusions turns on our opting for the broad construal of reasons for action. According to the narrow construal, a fact to the effect that A's V-ing would be good in a way is a reason for A to V only if A wants to do something good in that way. Similarly, a fact to the effect that A's not-V-ing would be bad in a way is a reason for A to V only if A wants to avoid doing something bad in that way. For example, the fact that A's not-V-ing would be unjust or miserly is a reason

75

for *A* to *V* only if *A* wants to avoid injustice or miserliness. As I said in Part I, section 13, this narrow construal of reasons for action strikes me as out of accord with our ideas about reasons for action.

But as I also said, I see no theoretically important reason for rejecting this narrow construal. Or for opting for it. Whatever we wish to accomplish in moral theory had better be accomplishable whether we opt for this narrow construal of reasons for action or for the broad one. There is something interesting that motivates opting for the narrow one, and I will discuss it in the following section. It is enough for our purposes to notice here that whether we call the kinds of facts I pointed to above "reasons for *A* to *V*" does not really matter. Some of them are—or together with (Isolation) are—conclusive reasons for believing that *A* ought to *V*. *That* is the point important to moral theory.

11.

Why is it that many contemporary moral philosophers have focused on the concept 'reason for action'? Why do many of them think, in particular, that *A* ought to *V* if and only if *V*-ing is what there is most reason for *A* to do? I suggest that that is because they wish to have it turn out that it is always *rational* for a person to do what he ought. Indeed, that rationality requires doing what one ought.

They swim upstream, however. That is because there is a familiar, because attractive, theory of rationality in action according to which *A*'s *V*-ing would be rational if and only if it would satisfy *A*'s wants. More precisely: if and only if it would satisfy *A*'s appropriately restricted wants. As I said in section 3, the restriction excludes merely passing wants, wants due to ignorance, and wants due to improper preference-bending. As I also said in section 3, the fact that *A*'s *V*-ing would satisfy *A*'s appropriately restricted wants cannot be thought sufficient to mark *A*'s *V*-ing as good for him. But it is no surprise that many people suppose that fact is sufficient to mark A's V-ing as rational.

If one accepts this familiar theory of rationality in action, then one cannot plausibly also accept that it is always rational for a person to do what he ought. For it is wildly implausible to suppose that wherever a person ought to do a thing, it will also be the case that his doing it would satisfy his wants—even if we appropriately restrict his wants.

So those many contemporary moral philosophers who think that A ought to V if and only if V-ing is what there is most reason for A to do—and think this because they wish to have it turn out that it is always rational for a person to do what he ought—have a hard job ahead of them. They need to find an alternative to that familiar theory of rationality in action.

Its very attractiveness is in fact what motivates opting for the narrow construal of reasons for action, according to which a fact is not a reason for action unless the agent has the appropriate wants—thus, for example, that the fact that A's V-ing would be good in a certain way is a reason for A to V only if A wants to do something good in that way. If one accepts that familiar theory of rationality in action, then one is very likely to think that a fact is a reason for A to V only if A's acting on it would conduce to the satisfying of A's wants. Moral philosophers who think that A ought to V if and only if V-ing is what there is most reason for A to do need to be able to reject the narrow construal of reasons for action; so (to repeat) they need to find an alternative to that familiar theory of rationality in action.

There surely is some pressure on us, whatever our views about reasons for action, to find an alternative. After all, it would be at a minimum unfortunate to have to agree that Alfred's paying his grocer's bill is irrational if his wants would be better satisfied if he did not. Moreover, we give advice when we say "You ought"; how can it be thought coherent to advise Alfred to pay his grocer's bill in the words "You ought to pay it, though I grant that your paying it would be irrational"?

But what alternative is available? One possibility begins by fixing on the fact that we are taking "ought" to have only one advice sense. We are supposing that its one advice sense is 'all things considered', where among the things considered is what would be good or bad for the agent. And it might be asked: "How could it be rational to believe that you ought (in that sense) to do a thing, and yet not do it?"[11] One obvious objection to the idea that this couldn't be rational is rebuttable. Thus suppose someone objects that a person might perfectly well believe he ought to do a thing and yet not want to do it, and therefore not do it. A friend of this idea replies: "I don't deny that this is possible, I say only that it is irrational."

Curiously enough, support for the idea can be found in a phenomenon observable in many of those who accept the familiar theory of rationality in action. What I refer to is the fact that they are inclined to resist the idea that a person ought to do a thing when, as it turns out, it would be (on the familiar theory) irrational for him to do it. They are inclined to say that if it would be irrational for the person to do the thing, then it is at a minimum doubtful that he ought to do it. *Nobody* is happy to allow that it might be true to say to Alfred: "You ought to pay your grocer's bill, though your paying it would be irrational."

My own impression, however, is that it just is not clear enough what the dispute between those who accept the familiar theory of rationality in action and those who are in search of an alternative is a dispute *about*. One way in which this unclarity emerges is the following.

Let us look again at reasons for belief. A fact F is a reason for believing a hypothesis H just in case F counts in favor of H. For

---

[11] I am grateful to Robert Streiffer for drawing my attention to this idea.

F to count in favor of *H* is for *F* to lend weight to *H*. And there is such a thing as a fact's being a conclusive reason for believing a hypothesis: *F* is a conclusive reason for believing *H* just in case *F* entails *H*. Suppose that *F* is a conclusive reason for believing *H*, and thus that *F* entails *H*. Then there is a quite clear sense in which it is 'against reason' for a person to believe that there is such a fact as *F*, while believing that *H* is false: it is self-contradictory to believe these things.

A fact *F* is a reason for *A* to *V* just in case *F* counts in favor of *A*'s *V*-ing. I suggested in Part I that for *F* to count in favor of *A*'s *V*-ing is for *F* to be a fact to the effect that *A*'s *V*-ing would be good in a way, or that *A*'s not *V*-ing would be bad in a way, or . . . Is there such a thing as a fact's being a conclusive reason for *A* to *V*? Suppose (i) we say that the fact that *A* ought to *V* is a conclusive reason for *A* to *V*. What could we mean by that? In what sense could it be thought to be 'against reason' for *A* to fail to *V* while believing that he ought to? Certainly no fact entails an action; what other sense is available?

I hasten to add that life is no easier for friends of the familiar theory of rationality in action. Suppose (ii) we say that the fact that *A*'s appropriately restricted wants would be satisfied if he *V*ed is a conclusive reason for *A* to *V*. What could we mean by that? In what sense could it be thought to be 'against reason' for *A* to fail to *V* while believing that his appropriately restricted wants would be satisfied if he *V*-ed?[12]

I think that it would pay to notice something further about the familiar theory of rationality in action. Suppose we accept the equally familiar Humean account of explanation of action. (I drew attention to it in Part I, section 11.) Thus suppose we

---

[12] The questions I am raising in the text here are also raised by the (in my view at best suspect) idea that there is such a thing as practical reasoning which contrasts with theoretical reasoning in the following way: while the conclusion of a bit of theoretical reasoning is a proposition, the conclusion of a bit of practical reasoning is an act.

accept that what a person will in fact do is what he believes will most efficiently satisfy his wants. Suppose, last, that Alfred's wants are all appropriately restricted, and that he believes that refraining from paying his grocer's bill will most efficiently satisfy them. The friend of the familiar theory of rationality says that for Alfred to pay his grocer's bill would be irrational. But that can't be right if Hume is right. For if Hume is right, then Alfred's paying his grocer's bill would not be irrational. It would be unintelligible. It would be inexplicable.

Moreover, if we say to Alfred "You ought to pay your grocer's bill," we are not advising him to do something it would be irrational for him to do. If Hume is right, we are instead advising him to do something his doing of which would be inexplicable. So be it. No doubt we do not give a person advice unless we think, or at least hope, that our doing so will affect his wants and thereby his actions. But alas it is not in the least uncommon for efforts of this kind to fail.

Yet isn't the familiar Humean account of explanation of action at least as attractive as the familiar theory of rationality in action?

There is much more to be said on this topic, but I suggest that we bypass it. For my own part, it seems to me good enough for the central purposes of a moral theorist if it should turn out—as I hope it has turned out—that some of the kinds of facts I pointed to earlier are conclusive reasons for *believing* that A ought to V. Whether they are therefore in some appropriate sense conclusive reasons for A to V is a question we can leave aside.

12.

The suggestions I have made obviously do not constitute a theory about what a person ought to do. What I have wanted to do is only to set out some features of the structure that I think such a theory should have. It should take account of the multiplicity of the ways of being good and bad, and it should tell us how the ways of being good and bad bear on what a person ought to do. The resulting theory would of course be more complex than Consequentialism, but that is only to be expected.

Filling the structure in requires supplying an account of what rights people have, and what makes it the case that they have them. I have said almost nothing about that here; I have simply helped myself to the notion of a right, in my characterization of justice and injustice in particular.[13]

More generally, it requires supplying an account of what marks an act as giving or failing to give adequate weight to the interests of all affected by it. I have no such account.

On the other hand, I think it unclear what such an account would have to look like—that is, how much precision should be expected of it. Comparisons between gains by one person and losses by another are notoriously difficult. Extreme examples are easy enough to construct: if Alfred gains relief from a sore throat, he gains something, but if Bertha loses her life, she loses markedly more. How much more can be said than that that difference is *sufficiently great* to mark as miserly an act by Alfred by which he relieves his sore throat with a drug he could easily have given to Bertha, who needs it for life? Again, injustice is breach of a non-overridden right, and the question whether a right is non-overridden turns on how stringent the right is, and how good for others infringing the right would be. Extreme examples are easy enough to construct: Bertha's right to not be killed by another is very stringent, and the fact that Alfred would gain relief from a sore throat by an act by which he would kill Bertha does not override Bertha's right.

There plainly is much room for differences in opinion about what counts as giving adequate weight to the interests of all who would be affected. The kind of theory I see the need of cannot be

---

[13] My own account of these matters appears in *The Realm of Rights*.

expected to contain an algorithm for settling such disputes. It has to be allowed to contrast much and little, and to invite us to attend to, and to argue by analogy from, particular cases in which it is clear on any view that a gain by one would be large and a loss to another would be small.

Moreover, it seems to me that such a theory should leave open the possibility that some such differences in opinion are not settleable at all. Not just that there may be nothing that will bring the parties to a dispute to come to agreement with each other; rather, more strongly, that there may be no correct answer to the question under dispute. The fact that there are such disputes on moral matters (if there are) should trouble us no less than does the fact that there are unsettleable disputes on nonmoral matters. No less, but also no more.

If we take practical reasoning to be reasoning about what to do, then conducting it well requires making exactly those more-or-less delicate contrasts between much and little and arguing by analogy from them. Allowing for the possibility of unsettleability is allowing for the possibility that in some cases, no conclusion can be shown to be correct. But that leaves plenty of room for cases in which conclusions are reachable—and I see no good reason to think that we are incapable of reaching them when they are.

Comments

COMMENT

❧

Philip Fisher

I N HER NUANCED and carefully argued clearing of the ground, Judith Thomson has set us down within Utilitarianism and proceeded to disable the machinery of Utilitarianism. While accomplishing this, she has raised a set of issues alongside her argument that are, in many cases, as provocative as the explicit argument itself.

Utilitarianism, since the time of Bentham, has carried with it features of its original purpose as a theory of legislation; that is: a public sphere ethical account whose core instance might be said to be governmental action affecting large numbers of people, most commonly by proposing, deliberating, passing, and putting into effect a new law. The new state of the world brought about by a broad-based income tax or by universal military conscription could be said to be the natural object of contemplation by legislators. They must consider something like the question of the greatest happiness of the greatest number because what they do changes the lives, directly or indirectly, of all citizens. Such new laws have as their situational presupposition what is often called a "crying need," a widely acknowledged problem to which citizens or interest groups among the larger population demand attention and action.

That is to say that there is, for a legislator, no general habit or interest in asking whether we should or should not do this or that, pass a law, change the world, or imagine whether on the whole the world would be better or worse off if we did this or that. There is instead the strongly driving force of a "crying need" somewhere that causes the Utilitarian legislative machinery to begin to function. Should there be universal health care legislation in America? Should official documents and forms be printed only in English? Should the sale of certain firearms be restricted? Finally, when we speak of a new condition of the world we mean only the world of these citizens who have existence as a common endeavor in one nation governed by these and no other laws.

When today, two hundred years after Bentham, we situate ourselves inside Utilitarian thinking, it is usually to take up private actions, what we might think of as Domestic Utilitarianism. Nevertheless, we bring to our inquiry the strongly marked features of the public sphere that I have begun by describing, even if they remain hidden in the shadows. Judith Thomson has, it seems to me, implicitly pushed this background issue of Utilitarianism into the foreground by her repeated use of the example of Alfred pressing the doorbell. The provocation of this instance lies in challenging us to ask, first of all, about the extent of ethics as a domain; secondly, about the use of isolated, freestanding examples, cases or instances as our entry point into ethical thinking; third, about Consequentialism applied to insignificant actions or to what we might call fragments of action. We could describe the act of pressing the doorbell as insignificant or we might want to observe that it has to be seen as a fragment of a larger story. This would lead us to ask a question about philosophical strategy. Why do we not begin with the larger story of which this is clearly a nested detail? Over time the withheld details of one or another larger story are gradually released for our inspection, but we are certain from the first appearance of this detail, that there exists some larger picture, and that what we are looking at when we picture the pressing of the doorbell is a only detail, and not a picture. We might ask why we are required to contemplate and to give a verdict on an as-yet-unstated full case.

An intriguing question is raised by confining our sight to Alfred pressing the doorbell. Alfred at the door raises the issue: How much ethics do we want? Can every (or even most) actions be evaluated as good? Or could it be that only a small percentage of all human actions have any ethical content, even though all have consequences? Alfred rings the bell. I lift my hand from the table. I sell my car. I move to Texas. How many, if any, of these actions should be part of ethics and part of our questions about the good?

As a second question we might ask: Do actions have to be scaled before ethics is found, just as in the physical world it turns out that there is only "something" at certain scales; in between there is nothing at all. I visited my friend who is sick in bed to bring him something to cheer him up. This is a description of an action at a certain scale. I spent my summer in Canada. That is at a different scale, both temporally and because it would commonly unpack to list many nested actions before we could say much about the encompassing fact of spending a summer in Canada. I rang a doorbell. That is a third scale. Neurons fired in a certain sequence in my central nervous system at a certain instant. All of these scales can be nested within one another and be parts of one another. Let us say that it was in Canada last summer that I learned an old friend was ill and visited him, and, in paying my visit, rang his doorbell and in ringing the doorbell the sequence of neurons fired in my central nervous system. But are they all of ethical interest? Are attributes like being good or bad only attributes of some, or one, but not of most or all scales nested around the same action? The atoms of an orange are not orange-colored atoms. These questions about the scale of ethical action and the small or large percentage of all actions that are suitable for ethical concern make up the first challenge present in this everyday instance.

Now I will look for a moment at the legislative background to our asking questions at all about certain things and not about others. We attend to Alfred's pressing the doorbell and its consequences, not out of mere curiosity, but because we want to know "whether he ought to press the doorbell or not." Because, in other words, it is not an act but an act in question, an act pictured prior to its execution, and subject to two possible paths. Ought he to press the bell and bring the world into being that will result, or refrain from pressing and bring another quite different world into being? A question and a choice. Every act, as T. S. Eliot's Prufrock worried, "disturbs the universe." But how, we might ask, did such an act as Alfred's come to be in question? The legislative background of Utilitarianism casts a strange shadow over what I have called Domestic Utilitarianism.

It may seem to us now a natural detail of the modern Anglo-American philosophical tradition that it brings each issue into the form of an assertion or a proposition:

I would like to assert that A is better than B

About this assertion we can ask if it is valid or invalid. In the background or prior to the moment of assertion is the more interesting moment, in which we are concerned with how something became a question, how an act stepped out of the flow of experience and became questionable:

Is this good?
Ought he to go the sickbed of his brother?
Ought Alfred to press the doorbell?

88

Only a few things in the flow of experience become questions, and within different systems quite different things turn up to face us as questions. What we would normally want to say of most isolated, everyday actions is that this particular act is not in question and never comes up as a question. Most things do not give rise to questions. Most actions are never regarded as isolated or freestanding. If we think of those rare things that do become questions, and ask why it is that in many other political or cultural circumstances they are not regarded as questions at all, then we would have to say that it might be a different question that needs to be asked. Those few things that can be thought of as being, as we say, "in question" arise within an extensive field of the tacit, the automatic, the habitual, the unthinkable, the customary, the already or long ago settled: all that is processed or done smoothly, acted on without decision or deliberation. Further, it may necessarily be part of the nature of many acts that they are not in question and are never or rarely subject to consciousness.

Why, we might ask, is it the "interrogative moment" and its aftermath of deliberation, dispute, uncertainty—the moment when we cannot go smoothly forward—that is taken to be the salient by which we want to grasp behavior in general, the good or goodness in general, since obviously the largest territory of ethical behavior, judgment, preference, and value is made up of the opposite, that which is not in question or is even unthinkable to picture as occurring as a question. In fleeing from a burning house one of the many things that does not occur as a question would be: Should I save my lamp or my child? If that occurred as a question or a deliberation or as something subject to the question Which is better? or What ought I to do? then we would say that the asking of this question in the pause before I acted showed, in fact, not keen ethical sensibility but some deleterious mystification of the ethical, some location outside the ethical altogether. That would be true no matter which way the question were answered. Nor could I present myself triumphantly to my friends by pointing out that after careful reflection I chose to save the child.

The important point is this: If what comes up to us as a question is only a small and very special detail of what counts as the whole domain of the ethical, are we able to learn about the geography of the ethical by this means?

Alfred is not only pressing the doorbell, he is in question and his act is in question. To begin at the site of the question might be one of the features of nonlegislative Utilitarianism and of recent Anglo-American philosophy that should attract our interest. Vast territories of already confident action and (therefore) embedded judgment and agreement lie behind the moment of the questionable, and so we might ask if it is by means of the leverage of the question that we can best gain access to the wider domain as a whole, or if we have chosen a corridor into the room of Ethics that in the end exposes an odd and mystifying perspective on the contents once we arrive there. We can say that in Public Utilitarianism there was always the notion of "pressing public questions" to which thinking came as a response, and after much thinking and deliberation, legislative action. There was no idea of choosing a detail of public life and just putting it in question.

In addition to isolated freestanding examples or cases like Alfred at the doorbell joined as it is to the moment of putting something in question, we have other alternatives for possible entry points into general ethical questions. There are also habits, rules, unexamined patterns of behavior, manners, widespread cultural things done, and those steady pressures that Hume called calm passions. Above all, there is the category not of isolated, freestanding, one-time events—like Alfred at the doorbell—but that of ongoing series of actions that cannot be seen individually or taken as freestanding, self-contained actions. Can ethical life and the ethical as a broad category be *first known* by questions which suppose problems and by places where the norms of unquestioned action (including all that is ruled out without even mentioning it or thinking of it) have broken down, creating for the first time a pause, a question, an uncertain space within a large, uncomplicated space of action and path taking?

As a more urgent consideration we have to say: If most ethical life goes on among people who live their lives together joined through family relations or as lovers, neighbors, friends, then the freestanding example cannot let us understand very much about this larger and more central territory of ethical life or ethical behavior. Any question about Albert is a question about an unknown stranger whom we first meet by means of this example. Isolated examples have as their presupposition the actions of strangers. Do we need instead necessary, familiar sequences of generosity, cruelty, selfishness, sacrifice, fairness, and harm between two friends, two sisters, two next-door neighbors, two business partners? Actions in a series, such as those between children who play together every day, or next-door neighbors, or soldiers in a platoon on the front line together day after day, or husbands and wives, or parents and their teenage children are not usually freestanding events that can be known or evaluated in isolation.

Actions in a series describe an ethical domain existing on a maintenance basis; that is, an ongoing world of known persons for whom I care and who will make up my future as well as constituting already a stock of past experiences—those with whom we are *in relation* (both relations of a natal kind, and relations of a chosen or contractual kind such as friendship, love, associates, partners, neighbors are examples of persons with whom we are maintaining something together—family life, a household, a business, a neighborhood, a team, etc.) It is only in legislation and in the public sphere that we all count equally as citizens, maintaining together our civic life. For the legislator the best example is to consider "anyone at all," the stranger, the freestanding instance and person. Alfred, for example.

In relation means in ongoing relation having a past, a present, and a future along with an archive of mutually affecting events as well as a number of situations of joint endeavor in which, for example, it would not usually be possible for the happiness of one person to occur as an outcome mixed with the deep unhappiness of the other because the very happiness of either one would be limited if not destroyed by the simultaneous deep unhappiness of the other. A whole family prospers or goes bankrupt. An unhappy marriage is not the simple sum of the states of the two individuals in which although one is happy and the other unhappy, the greater quantity of unhappiness on the one side outweighing the smaller happiness on the other.

I will now turn from the legislative background to a second issue, the relation of Consequentialism to what I call the radius of the will. Thomson, early in Part I, gives the following summary: "We may suppose that Alfred's pressing the doorbell caused many other events to occur. Thus, his pressing the doorbell caused a circuit to close, a bell to ring, a person inside to feel pleased, and so on and on." What do the words "and so on and on" mean? Do they mean something like the triple dots in a mathematical nonrepeating decimal? So on and so on and so on ever after? Why do we commonly evaluate only the proximate or the nearby field of action for events? Do we have any choice? The weak skepticism about Consequentialism, as Thomson defined it, concerned our doubt that we could *know* all that followed—literally, what the world would be like if Alfred acts. This, she points out, concerns only a question of fact, not of value.

We are ordinarily forced to operate with a notion that I call the "radius of the will." We have only a limited distance of concern in

making evaluations of acts. If, due to my negligence, my car strikes a pedestrian who as a result spends the rest of his life in a wheelchair, we say that my negligence results in this fact. But if we say "and so on and on," we have to ask if my negligence also causes the fact that his marriage breaks up after two years of strain that was, at least in part, a secondary consequence of the new conditions brought about by the accident that I caused. Or, in the other direction, does my negligence cause the fact that my victim, being mechanically gifted and forced to think long and hard about life in a wheelchair, invents a new wheelchair that improves the lives of thousands of people, or that, housebound, he spends a great deal of time with his young son, teaching him chess, among other things. The son, as a result, becomes a chess master, rising rapidly in tournament play until, defeated and humiliated in play by a bitter rival, he takes his life at age twenty-two, and so on and on. What is my part in these many and varied later events, all linked in some way to my negligence and the accident that resulted?

If causality and Consequentialism, unexpected as well as easily anticipated consequences, remote as well as proximate changes in how the world now stands after an event, include consequences for second-, third- and tenth-order persons, and if this is a normal truth about action, then "and so on and on" is one of the most powerful phrases in our vocabulary. Nineteenth-century novels like those of Dickens, Tolstoy, George Eliot, and Balzac reach enormous length, sometimes nine hundred pages or more, because of an interest in just this question of multiplied and varied consequences seen through a long-term view of time and causality in experience.

Notice that as soon as we move outside the radius of the will we encounter a rude challenge to simple praise or blame or to any attempt to speak of an action as good or bad. This problem lay at the heart of what in theology was called the *felix culpa*, or "fortunate fall." If Adam and Eve's fall made possible so much later good, was all subsequent good a result of that sin? Is the improved wheelchair design a result of my negligence as a driver, since that negligence confined my victim to a wheelchair and gave him the time to think about its limitations and invent an improved version? Outside theology the same challenge of complex outcomes lies at the heart of the moral notion of dramatic irony. When we move the frame of attention out to the next-on scale of time or inclusiveness of persons, and then do so again and again, we are likely at each step to face what Aristotle called "reversals" rather than incremental or integrable effects. What is a bad overall outcome at stage one becomes a good overall outcome at stage two, mixed but tending to bad at three, disastrous at four, tragic at five, redemptive and angelic at six. Any and all sequences and combinations are both possible and common. It is notable that in adding detail after detail as she presents her example, Judith Thomson chooses the added detail so as to impose Aristotelian reversals and dramatic irony on her hidden but slowly unfolded larger story.

The mischief of dramatic irony is one of the moral secrets hidden within the words "and so on and on." As is the theological, totalizing question of the fortunate fall once we pass beyond the first consequences of eating the apple: expulsion from Eden. With the ever larger radius of consequences within action we encounter once again the unwelcome philosophical guest: the necessary hold over us (and over our thinking) of the proximate and the nearby. It was this same hold of the nearby that we encountered earlier in thinking of the persons with whom we are in ongoing relations in an habitual world of actions in a series, rather than the freestanding moment or instance placed in question whether in the political and legislative world of traditional

Utilitarianism or its domestic equivalent in questions about the isolated act of an unknown person, like Albert pressing the doorbell.

Finally, I would like to step outside these features of Utilitarianism and of modern Anglo-American philosophy that I have singled out, and turn to the larger matter of alternative starting points.

We might always ask: Why have we chosen the point of entry that we have for ethical thinking, and what are the consequences of that choice? What is the best point of entry for ethical reflection?

(1) Is it the case or the example? The case confronts us with an already completed action where we picture ourselves as a jury or judge expected to render a verdict, whether praise or blame, punishment or reward. In legal terms, a case is self-contained, isolated for attention, and we place ourselves in the position of "anyone"—a fellow citizen, and the agents (victim and accused) are strangers to us—unknown, or as we could say "any fellow citizen."

(2) Is it the choice or decision that I must make about what to do next? Including reflection and the weighing of alternatives just prior to an act?

(3) Is it legislative? Public deliberation about laws or rules affecting all citizens and future possible actions? Or rules within smaller groups like neighborhood associations or clubs where these rules will apply to all members? Or even family rules involving children?

(4) Is it the ordering and rational defense of our philosophical explanations of our general principles of behavior converting them into ethical theory, with consistency and

the search for a few most general principles underlying cases, choices, legislative actions?

(5) Is it the transmission to the next generation in processes of education, habit building, formation and deformation of character? Transmission is achieved by selective emphasis and partial forgetting—both explicit and inexplicit—by rules and by transmission through personal example (commented upon or not) by models (both negative and positive) or even without pointing to anything about models by your choice of the people included regularly in family life and its events or mostly excluded from that life.

(6) Is it by language? The words or terms we use and how we use them, assuming this provides us with a widely shared distilled set of aspects or core applications.

Whichever starting point we choose casts forward a structure over subsequent thinking, even once that starting point has been forgotten or come to seem natural and inevitable. It is this latter condition that I have looked at here in these remarks on Thomson's "Goodness and Advice."

COMMENT

Martha C. Nussbaum

1.

Thomson's subtle analysis begins from the description of a problem: people have confident moral beliefs, but they lack confidence that they have good reason to hold that those beliefs are true. To get past this impasse by proposing a reasonable account of moral requirement is the overall aim of Thomson's project. In Part I, she turns first to a very plausible candidate, the Utilitarian account of what one ought to do. She analyzes the Utilitarian account, arguing that it relies on two distinct theses: a substantive thesis about the good, typically some version of Hedonism, and a thesis that Thomson calls Consequentialism, and which she defines as follows: "A person ought to do a thing if and only if the world will be better if he does it than if he does any of the other things it is open to him to do at the time." The rest of Part I is devoted to the critical examination of the Consequentialist thesis. Thomson argues that it rests on a very implausible view about goodness; once we understand that all goodness is goodness in a way, and that there are many distinct ways of being good, the entire project of maximizing the good loses its appeal, and even its coherence.

I find what Thomson says about goodness subtle and convincing. Given the brevity of this reply, I must therefore focus on the areas of disagreement. I shall argue that there are some significant differences between the Moorean version of Consequentialism that Thomson attacks and some other prominent modern versions of Consequentialism. These differences, I shall argue, are such that while Thomson's argument is a very powerful argument against Moore, it does not yet undermine these more recent projects. Whether they succeed or not, more argument is needed. I shall then make some further remarks about the relationship between Utilitarianism and Consequentialism. Finally, turning to one piece of Thomson's Part II, I shall argue that the problem of moral dilemmas is a more serious one that Thomson believes it to be. There are good ethical reasons why philosophers should give these dilemmas a place of prominence that Thomson denies them, and build a recognition of their significance into an account of moral requirement. This recognition illuminates significant issues about both private and public choice.

2.

Thomson defines Consequentialism as the thesis that "a person ought to do a thing if and only if the world will be better if he does it than if he does any of the other things it is open to him to do at the time." This definition diverges in interesting ways from some standard definitions of Consequentialism. I shall argue that Thomson has loaded the dice: it is because of some particular features of Thomson's definition of Consequentialism (not unfamiliar, to be sure, and securely grounded in Moore) that Consequentialism entails the thesis about the unity of the good that she rightly finds implausible. Defined in a different way, Consequentialism can survive her insightful argument. More important, there are some good prima facie reasons to embrace a Consequentialism that is not committed to an implausible form of monism about the good.

In what follows I do not commit myself to Consequentialism. I believe that there are many arguments to be pursued before one would have determined whether a form of Consequentialism can survive all the major objections that can be brought against the view. And, as will be seen, I have my suspicions that the most plausible and capacious versions of Consequentialism may make so many adjustments that Consequentialism no longer remains a distinctive type of ethical theory. My intention is only to establish that Thomson has not yet marshaled all the arguments that would be necessary to defeat the most plausible versions of Consequentialism now before us.

So let us look at some standard accounts. Philip Pettit, for example, begins his recent collection of essays on Consequentialism with the following definition: "Roughly speaking, Consequentialism is the theory that the way to tell whether a particular choice is the right choice for an agent to have made is to look at the relevant consequences of the decision; to look at the relevant effects of the decision on the world."[1] Similarly, Amartya Sen and Bernard Williams define Consequentialism as the thesis "that actions are to be chosen on the basis of the states of affairs which are their consequences."[2] Notice that these definitions, unlike Thomson's, do not give any detailed account of *how* the resulting states of affairs are to be evaluated; in particular, they make no reference to a choice that makes the world better than any other available option.

There are many reasons to embrace Consequentialism defined in this general and intuitive way. Such a Consequentialism need not be motivated by any implausible view about the unity of the good. Instead, it can be sufficiently motivated by resistance to a certain type of deontological rigorism—by the idea that people

---

[1] Philip Pettit, ed., *Consequentialism* (Aldershot: Dartmouth, 1993), p. xiii.

[2] Amartya Sen and Bernard Williams, eds., introduction to *Utilitarianism and Beyond* (Cambridge: Cambridge University Press, 1982), Introduction, 3–4. They note that the term was introduced in Elizabeth Anscombe's famous article "Modern Moral Philosophy," *Philosophy* 33 (1958): 1–19.

who are about to act should focus on taking responsibility for the consequences of their actions, rather than saying, let me follow my duty even if the world should end.

Consider the debate between Krishna and Arjuna in the *Mahabharata*.[3] Krishna says that Arjuna should follow his military duty in the civil war without thinking of the devastation he is about to bring on his family and his nation by killing half of his relatives. Arjuna, by contrast, says that all the consequences have to be weighed: that one will have done one's duty is only one part of those consequences, not the whole.[4] Notice, here, that Arjuna does not insist on any notion of the unity or homogeneity of good; nor does he deny the importance of deontological requirements. He simply says that one should look at the entirety of the consequences, including one's own violation of duty. Arjuna is not certain about how to rank the alternatives actually before him, since they contain serious bad features that are not easily made commensurable: violation of duty on the one hand, the killing of most of one's relatives on the other. But he can at least say this: a situation in which one does one's duty and one does not kill one's relatives is certainly preferable to a situation in which one does one's duty and one does kill one's relatives. Krishna's narrow focus on duty alone prevents him from seeing what is extremely bad about the choices that Arjuna faces. We might call Arjuna's brand of Consequentialism "Sensible Consequentialism": that is, a view that makes no implausible claims about the good, but still remains determined to evaluate choices in the light of the totality of the consequences they produce.

---

[3] This example is used in a similar connection by Amartya Sen in "Rights and Duties," Heffers Lecture, Cambridge University, 27 November 1998. I am grateful to Sen for permission to refer to and (later) to quote from this lecture.

[4] That it is a part is another central claim of Sen's lecture: he insists that the special involvement of the agent in the action can and must be included in the description of the consequences.

An example structurally similar to Arjuna's dilemma was famously given by Kant in his essay on the alleged duty to lie from altruistic motives. Kant holds that one should never violate the duty not to lie, even when a murderer is at the door and is asking about the whereabouts of his would-be victim. Almost everyone who reads this essay turns Consequentialist at this point, feeling that Kant, like Krishna, has allowed a narrow focus on duty to blind him to a morally central feature of the case. Most of us, without any commitment to the homogeneity of the good, feel that the Kantian agent's failure to consider the totality of the consequences of his choice is morally heinous. If he lies to the murderer, one part of the consequences surely is the fact that he will have violated a duty. But another part, outweighing this one for the Sensible Consequentialist, is that a person will live who would otherwise die. No matter what outweighs, it is at least important that he make the choice with the totality of the consequences in view.

Notice that, corresponding to Sensible Consequentialism, there are also sensible deontologies, which allow the chooser to consider the consequences so long as the decision is not made on the basis of consequences alone. Kant's rigorist position is not common among deontologists, and has been extensively criticized from within deontology itself. Sometimes the criticism takes the form of emphasizing the fact that there is more than one deontological requirement on the scene in such cases: in this case, the duty not to lie conflicts with the duty to protect one's friend. I shall discuss such cases in section 5 below. Sometimes, however, the example is construed as one where one ought to consider not only a deontological requirement, but the consequences of obeying that requirement as well. A theory may count as deontological provided that the consequences are not the only thing that the theory considers. These complex alternatives, as I shall argue, run into one another and become hard to distinguish from one another. It is indeed difficult, as we shall see, to say which positions are deontological and which are Consequentialist, once one sensibly takes these complexities into account.

Sensible Consequentialism is especially attractive as a thesis about public morality. We are all familiar with public actors who make a great point of purity and duty without asking about the totality of the consequences of their acts; others, by contrast, ask about the overall consequences of a choice for the whole group. Which do we prefer, the Krishnas or the Arjunas? I think there are reasons to prefer Arjuna. We want public actors to think about their duties and the morality of their acts, but we also want them to put that thought into a larger context, thinking about all the different types of consequences their choices may have. Take just one example: both Cicero and Kant hold that it is always wrong to lie to the enemy in wartime, or to use spies. The Sensible Consequentialist I have imagined would not hold to this idea come hell or high water. If only good spying would save the whole nation from destruction, it should be preferred (as Grotius saw), despite its morally unsavory character.

But I have so far ducked what for Thomson must be the central issue: how, exactly, does this Sensible Consequentialist perform the evaluation of consequences, if not by reference to an implausible thesis about the good? It is here that the specific content of Thomson's definition must be scrutinized. Thomson, it will be remembered, defines Consequentialism in terms of the choice that makes the world better than it would have been had one made any other available choice. In other words, she demands the optimal choice, and this, in turn, apparently requires a complete ranking of outcomes. Here is where I feel that the deck has been unfairly stacked against the Consequentialist: for the Sensible Consequentialist need not say that a complete ranking is available. She probably does need to rely on some intuitive idea of getting more good rather than less. But she need not require that the agent make the *best* among the available choices: she need only require that the agent make a choice that is, at any rate, *no worse than* the other available alternatives—in other words, *no other option is better*.

This small shift, from *the best* to the idea that nothing else is *better*, is by now a standard feature of discussions of Consequentialism. In a fine recent article, David Sosa begins his examination of Consequentialism with the following definition:

> (C): It is *right* to S to do A (S *ought* to do A or S *should do A*) if no total state of affairs that would be a consequence of S's doing any alternative to A would be better than the total state of affairs that would be a consequence of S's doing A.[5]

The crucial point is this: To say that no other option is better, I need not have before me a complete ranking of the options. And it is only if I demand a complete ranking of the options that I am coerced into an implausible thesis about the unity of good.

Let me illustrate this point by talking about Sen's view, since there are not many non-utilitarian Consequentialists, and he is an eminent one.[6] In a recent lecture on the topic of Consequentialism,[7] Sen has added to his earlier thin definition the observation that, as typically understood, Consequentialism does involve not only the idea of looking to consequences, but also an idea of maximizing. But it is extremely important, he continues, to understand that maximizing is not the same thing as optimizing. Maximization, that is, does not require that all alternatives be comparable, and does not even require that a best alternative be identifiable. Maximization requires only that we do not choose an

---

[5] David Sosa, "Consequences of Consequentialism," *Mind* 102 (1993): 101–22.

[6] Another important contribution to this area of ethical theory is John Broome, *Weighing Goods* (Oxford: Basil Blackwell, 1991), especially chap. 1.

[7] "Rights and Duties."

alternative that is *worse than* another that is available. "If we cannot compare and rank two alternatives, then choosing either from that pair would satisfy the requirement of maximization." Sen notes that in informal usage the term "maximization" is used in many ways, leading to some confusion on this point. Some people clearly do use the word to mean what he means by "optimizing," namely, going for the *best* among the alternatives. But he then notes standard mathematical definitions of maximization (for example, by Bourbaki in set theory and by Gerard Debreu in axiomatic economic analysis[8]), clearly distinguishing between maximizing and optimizing: optimizing requires the existence of a best alternative (though not a uniquely best alternative); maximizing does not. The two coincide when an ordering is complete, but not when a complete ordering is unavailable. If, for example, there is an incompleteness so that *A* and *B* cannot be ranked vis-à-vis each other, but each of them is better than all the available alternatives, maximizing would require choosing either *A* or *B*.

Sen at this point seems to me to go wrong, by confusing the absence of a complete ranking with a tie. For he remarks that the puzzle known as Buridan's ass is no problem for the maximizer, though it is for the optimizer. The donkey sees two haystacks which it cannot rank vis-à-vis each other, and therefore starves. But if the donkey had been a maximizer, it would have understood that going toward either haystack was better than starving, and his maximizing strategy would have permitted him to choose either one. So: the absence of a complete ranking does not prevent choice. Sen is wrong, however, to assimilate the Buridan's ass problem to the problem of incomplete ranking. The donkey's problem is that there is a tie. Both haystacks are equally good. And here it seems that Thomson's reply is exactly right: if there

[8] Sen refers to N. Bourbaki, *Éléments de Mathématique* (Paris: Harmann, 1939), *Theory of Sets*, English translation 1968; Gerard Debreu, *The Theory of Value* (New York: Wiley, 1959). I take this on trust from Sen.

is a tie, the Moorean (Optimizing) Consequentialist need not be stymied (as Sen suggests): he can simply say that the donkey "need not, but may, do either."

So Sen is wrong to think that ties are a serious problem for the Optimizing Consequentialist, or a reason to prefer maximizing over optimizing. But his defense of maximizing over optimizing is not thereby undermined, because he is also wrong to say that the Buridan's ass case is the kind of case that most revealingly shows the difference between his theory and the Moorean type of theory. The cases that do show the superiority of the maximizing strategy are cases where there are a number of options that can be seen to be better than other available options, *but these options cannot be ranked at all among one another*. What could such cases be? What Sen has in mind, throughout his work on this topic, are cases in which the goods involved are plural and incommensurable, in such a way that there is no plausible way of ranking the options against one another. Let us say that I have a hundred dollars. I can (a) give it to a needy friend; or (b) give it to Oxfam; or (c) flush it down the toilet; or (d) buy myself a luxurious dinner. A Sen-type Consequentialist could argue here that (a) and (b) are clearly superior to (c), and almost certainly to (d) as well. But one might plausibly hold that it is not possible to rank (a) against (b) because the goods of friendship are too different from the goods of famine relief. Now, some Consequentialists would see a tie here, but I am concerned with one who would refuse to say that, who would say, "Where the goods are so different, I really cannot rank the options at all." This is a plausible thing to say, though it is not the only thing that one might say here (see section 3 below). And it certainly is what Sen would say in lots of cases of this kind. Thomson, so far as I can see, has given us no reasons for supposing that a Consequentialist cannot say this.

The point is that in such a case there is no *optimal* alternative, but there is a *maximal* alternative in Sen's sense. That is, there is no single best choice, but there are two choices that are clearly better than the available alternatives. Choosing (a), I am choosing something that is not *worse than* any other alternative, although I cannot say that it is exactly as good as the other one that remains on the agenda, because I have refused to rank them against one another. The idea is that *better than, worse than,* and *just as good as* all presuppose a way of ranking, and this is what I deny I can have, where (a) and (b) are concerned. Thus the Sen-type Consequentialist can say: I may do either (a) or (b), but both are preferable to (c) and (d).

Notice that this is the same answer that Thomson's Consequentialist will give on the basis of her account of ties, following Moore. But it is the same answer in appearance only, because reasons of quite a different sort underlie the conclusion in each case. Thomson's Consequentialist compares (a) and (b) and finds them to be equal in goodness; he says, "We have a tie on our hands." And that is why he says that one may choose either (a) or (b). Sen's Consequentialist says that we just can't rank (a) and (b) at all; all we can say is that they are both better than any of the other available alternatives. Thomson's Consequentialist may be committed to the homogeneity of the good, but Sen's is clearly not. Indeed, it is precisely the nonhomogeneity of the good that has led Sen to suppose that we can in many situations come up with at most a partial ranking.

In short, it is the demand for a complete ranking that runs us into trouble with the diversity in goodness. If we accept Thomson's powerful claim that there are many distinct types of goodness, and indeed that all goodness is goodness in a way, or in a context, then it seems implausible that we would ever get anywhere near completeness in the ranking of states of affairs. On the other hand, if we stick to the humbler maximizing (i.e., not worse than) sort of Consequentialism, we will still be able to order many states of affairs by their goodness. Suppose, for example, we identify three distinct ends that public policy in a nation should be promoting: let us say that they are health, education, and the protection of political liberties. Now we could show that these are distinct types of goods in Thomson's sense; they play different roles in people's lives, and it is implausible to think that there is one thing, the good, that they all contain. It seems to follow from this that we cannot in a general way rank them vis-à-vis each other, generating a complete ordering of the type required for Consequentialism as Thomson defines it. Nonetheless, says the Sensible Consequentialist, we can still order lots of outcomes, and we still have ample guidance for choice. For there are many outcomes that involve progress on all three fronts (that are Pareto-optimal), and these can clearly be ordered above the outcomes that involve regress on all three. Outcomes that involve progress on one front and stasis on two can also be preferred to outcomes involving stasis on all three, or progress on one and regress on two. And so forth. In short, incompleteness is not fatal to consequential analysis, and such a consequential analysis still has a lot to offer to public policy. Sen's Consequentialism certainly appears to offer less than the more ambitious Moorean variety. It is a humble view, and it may for that reason seem less interesting. But I have suggested that it is all the more interesting for being plausible.

There are many other issues we would need to consider before we would decide that such a Consequentialism was acceptable. One such issue would be whether Consequentialism so described can make sufficient place for the protection of rights. One central feature of Sen's work on this topic has been his determination to defend Consequentialism on this score, by arguing that we may build into the account of consequences the fact that rights have been protected (or, as the case may be, violated). Another such issue would be whether Consequentialism can make sufficient room for an agent's personal involvement with his or her own

action: the "integrity" point so well pressed against the Consequentialist by Bernard Williams. The fact that I have done a murder, said Williams, made that situation crucially different from a
situation in which murder is done, but I am not the doer. Once
again, Sen has defended Consequentialism here as well, saying
that one may include the agent's own special involvement in his
or her action as a part of what one evaluates when one evaluates
the consequences. Thus, if I murder someone, the fact that I will
have done a murder is a part of the consequences of my act; if a
murder happens without my participation, the fact I will have
done a murder does not show up in the consequences.

Clearly, we need to ponder these two replies of Sen's, to see
whether they really do handle the objections. And then we need
to ask a further question: if we accept all these moves as moves
within Consequentialism, is Consequentialism then any kind of
distinctive moral theory at all, or simply a formal way of organiz-
ing any moral theory that one might want to defend? The latter
position has been taken, for example, by James Dreier, when he
argues that any moral theory whatever may be "consequential-
ized," put into Consequentialist form; thus Consequentialism de-
livers nothing distinctive. It's just a bookkeeping device.[9]

It seems to me that a Consequentialist of Sen's variety really
does need to face this objection. For it may ultimately emerge
that Sen's Consequentialism is so broad that it really does not,
after all, fulfill its original ambition, which was to distinguish the
Arjunas from the Krishnas, offering a distinctive way of thinking
about how to act. After all, we can "consequentialize" Krishna's
view easily enough, following Dreier's suggestion, by saying that

[9] James Dreier, "Structures of Normative Theories," *Monist* (1993): 22–40, at 23: "The
main strategy for 'consequentializing' any given moral theory is simple. We merely take
the features of an action that the theory considers to be relevant, and build them into the
consequences. For example, if a theory says that promises are not to be broken, then we
restate this requirement: that a promise has been broken is a bad consequence."

for Krishna, the only relevant consequences are that duties will have been performed or not performed. The deaths of relatives just don't count for him as part of the relevant consequences. So we then have two different Consequentialist theories, with different accounts of the relevant consequences, not a difference between Consequentialism and some other type of theory. Then, it seems, Sen should find fault with Krishna not by saying that he should be a Consequentialist, but by saying that he has the wrong account of relevant consequences. But then the whole reason for Sen's preference for Consequentialism has just evaporated. We can't help being Consequentialists if we choose to keep the books that way, and we differ only about what we put into the account of relevant consequences.

I shall not pursue this issue here, although I believe that it is a difficult one indeed for Sen's very capacious theory. What it shows is that Consequentialism and deontology are not so easy to distinguish, and in the end the real work may not be done by such formal distinctions at all, but only by the more specific arguments given by each theory concerning what is of practical relevance. But I feel that it is not necessary to pursue these issues in this context: For we can see that Sen gets into this difficulty (if it is one) not by his defense of partial orderings alone, but by wanting to accommodate every single objection that philosophers have made to Consequentialism. There might certainly be something clearly recognizable as Consequentialism that did not accommodate every single one of these objections and thus was still a distinctive type of ethical theory, but one that, unlike Moore's, made room for partial orderings and noncomparability. This is the sort of Consequentialism I think Thomson needs to consider more seriously.[10]

[10] One such intermediate position, in which the plurality of the good is strenuously maintained but Sen's route of response to the Williams integrity objection is closed off, is John Broome's *Weighing Goods*, chap. 1.

In short: Thomson's focus on Moore exacts a cost. While rejecting a form of Consequentialism that has undoubtedly had currency in Utilitarianism, she ignores the form that the most prominent non-Utilitarian Consequentialists in contemporary political philosophy would defend.

3.

There is another issue that needs fuller consideration than it receives in Thomson's Part I, if we are to satisfy ourselves that the arguments for and against Consequentialism have been drawn up with sufficient subtlety. This is the difficult issue of the relationship between *comparability* and *commensurability*. Frequently we rank one option over another, saying, "This is better." Utilitarians standardly suggest that when we do so, we must be commensurating the alternatives in terms of some hidden metric of goodness. Our statement really reduces to the statement "This contains more good." It is this way of proceeding that Thomson correctly assails. She rightly holds that we may prefer one option to another without commensurating them along some single qualitative dimension. Saying that two options are thus *comparable* does not imply that they are *commensurable*, where that means measurable in terms of a single standard of value.[11]

But once we accept this, it seems to me that the Sensible Consequentialist has far more room to maneuver. Sen's theory suggests (although he nowhere, to my knowledge, argues this point) that where there are incommensurable goods, where, that is,

[11] For an attempt—I think misguided—to assimilate incommensurability to noncomparability, see Joseph Raz, *The Morality of Freedom* (Oxford: Clarendon Press, 1986), chap. 13; for argument that incommensurability does not imply noncomparability, see my *The Fragility of Goodness* (Cambridge: Cambridge University Press, 1986), chap. 10, on Aristotle; and Henry Richardson, *Practical Reasoning about Final Ends* (Cambridge: Cambridge University Press, 1994). For an excellent sifting of all dimensions of this question, see Ruth Chang, ed., *Incommensurability, Incomparability, and Practical Reason* (Cambridge: Harvard University Press, 1997).

there is no qualitatively homogeneous metric of goodness by which to compare the diverse alternatives before us, we cannot compare, hence rank, the alternatives at all. In short, Sen, like Joseph Raz, assimilates incommensurability to total incomparability. The only thing we can say at this point is that there is just no way of comparing, hence ranking, the alternatives. And that is why we are left with so many holes in the ordering. But if we do not make the Raz move, if we insist—I believe with Aristotle—that comparison between distinct and plural goods does not require a hidden metric of goodness, then we may actually be able to rank and order many more states of affairs than Sen thinks (though probably not all of them) without losing the plurality and genuine incommensurability of the good.

Obviously this is not an issue to be resolved in such a cursory examination. But, once again, it is one that we need to resolve if we are accurately to assess the problems and prospects of various forms of Consequentialism.

4.

I have a further issue to raise about the way in which Thomson defines Utilitarianism, and, thus, about the way she relates Utilitarianism and Consequentialism. For Thomson, Utilitarianism is the conjunction of Hedonism About Goodness with Consequentialism. But there is a third part to the standard Utilitarian picture that needs independent consideration. This is what is standardly called "sum-ranking": that is, in sorting out the rankings of alternatives, we simply *add up* individual utilities or pleasures.[12] As Sen and Williams remark, this really is a distinct feature: we might have ranked consequences, instead, by attending to the utility of the least well off, or the best off. Thus, as they remark, the economic interpretation of the Rawlsian Difference Principle

---

[12] See Sen and Williams, *Utilitarianism and Beyond*, p. 4.

is a type of welfarist Consequentialism that does not use sum-ranking: we look at the welfare (defined, here, in terms of primary goods rather than pleasure) of the least well off, rather than summing up, or averaging, everyone's welfare.

Recognizing the distinctness of sum-ranking as a component in Utilitarianism seems important if we want to keep what I have called Sensible Consequentialism around as an option for moral and political thought. For sum-ranking has some very objectionable consequences. As John Rawls has insisted, it treats people simply as inputs into an overall social function, and neglects, in significant ways, the separateness of each person's life. For example, if *A* is an extremely poor woman in rural Bihar, and *B* is a very rich businessman in Bombay, it funnels *A*'s pain into the same calculus as *B*'s pleasure, in such a way that *B*'s exceeding happiness cancels out *A*'s misery. This problem is caused not by hedonism, but by sum-ranking: it could have been generated using any account of social welfare one chooses. The point made repeatedly by Rawls and others is that this way of treating people does not respect them as persons: it encourages the idea that we can buy one person's happiness with another's pain, and thus in effect makes some people tools of the happiness of others. This is a truly important point, and it is, I believe, the most fundamental point in modern liberal critiques of Utilitarianism.

But notice that the culprit is sum-ranking, not Consequentialism. If we had adopted the Difference Principle as our account of how to perform a consequential evaluation of the relevant utilities, we would get a very different picture. So too, if one were to say, as I myself have, that those outcomes are better than others where all citizens are above a specifiable threshold on all the major goods.[13] That way of looking to consequences respects people and does not use them as the tools of others. So we should

[13] See *Women and Human Development: The Capabilities Approach* (Cambridge: Cambridge University Press, 2000).

not suppose that Consequentialism all by itself has these unpleasant features.

The Consequentialisms I have been investigating are not the Moorean version that Thomson attacks: in that sense there might seem to be little disagreement between us. But I think it is important to get clear about exactly where the problems lie. If we are to complete the assessment of Consequentialism as a type of ethical theory (or even to decide whether in fact it is a distinctive type of ethical theory), we have more work to do.

5.

For all her criticism of Utilitarianism, there is one way in which Thomson seems to me to remain too close to the Utilitarian picture, and not to take far enough her own insight into the diversity of the good.

If one thinks that the good is plural, then it is natural to suppose that there will be serious contingent conflicts of value, some of them involving moral values.[14] Agamemnon is told by Artemis that he must kill his daughter. Let us suppose that this command imposes an absolutely stringent moral requirement; but there is also an absolutely stringent moral requirement not to kill the daughter. The right thing to say here, it seems to me,[15] is that I

---

[14] I have discussed these conflicts in a number of places, particular *Fragility*, chaps. 2 and 3, and, most recently, in "The Costs of Tragedy: Some Moral Limits of Cost-Benefit Analysis," *Journal of Legal Studies* 29 (2000), 1005–36. In the contemporary philosophical literature on this issue, I have found most helpful: Ruth Barcan Marcus, "Moral Dilemmas and Consistency," *Journal of Philosophy* 77 (1980): 121–36; Bernard Williams, "Ethical Consistency," in *Problems of the Self* (Cambridge: Cambridge University Press, 1993), 166–86; John Searle, "*Prima Facie* Obligations," in *Philosophical Subjects: Essays Presented to P. F. Strawson*, ed. Z. van Straaten (Oxford: Clarendon Press, 1980), 238–59; Michael Stocker, *Plural and Conflicting Values* (New York: Oxford University Press, 1990); Michael Walzer, "Political Action: The Problem of Dirty Hands," *Philosophy and Public Affairs* 2 (1973): 160–80.

[15] See *Fragility*, chap. 2. And see now my Introduction to the revised edition of *Fragility* (Cambridge: Cambridge University Press, 2001), which discusses these conflicts further.

ought to obey the god and I ought to protect my daughter—but I can't do both. Whatever I do, I will be violating some genuine moral requirement. (Arjuna's situation seems similar.) Logically, we might represent this, as Bernard Williams does, by saying that "ought" is not agglomerative: "I ought to do A" and "I ought to do B" does not entail "I ought to do both A and B."[16] There may well be some all-things-considered way of deciding what I should actually do—for it's important to distinguish such tragic cases from cases where there is no way of choosing. In this case, given that disobeying the god also meant the death of all his troops, Agamemnon was well advised to kill his daughter. But the other "ought" still remains, undefeated. It is still the case that he ought not to kill her.

In short: in many situations of choice, there is not just one question to be asked, there are two. One is the obvious question: What should I do? But the other one, the one that I shall call the "tragic question" is the question "Is there any option available to me that is free of serious wrongdoing?" I am suggesting that the answer to the tragic question is sometimes "no," and that it is important to ponder this fact.

But what does this mean? Isn't it just moral squeamishness to say that there is an undefeated moral claim on the scene, even when an agent has chosen the best of the available alternatives? I would argue not. Even in a case like Agamemnon's, where the tragedy does not look like one that could have been avoided by better political planning, there is a point to the tragic question. It keeps the mind of the chooser firmly on the fact that his action is an immoral action, which it is always wrong to choose. The recognition that one has "dirty hands" is not just self-indulgence: it has significance for future actions. It informs the chooser that he may owe reparations to the vanquished, and an effort to rebuild

---

[16] Williams, "Ethical Consistency." Thomson suggests a subtly different strategy in note 10 of Part II.

their lives after the disaster that will have been inflicted on them. When the recognition is public, it constitutes an acknowledgment of moral culpability, something that frequently has significance in domestic and international politics.[17] (Michael Walzer writes eloquently about Hiroshima in this regard.) Most significantly, it reminds the chooser that he must not do such things henceforth, except in the very special tragic circumstance he faces here. Slaughtering one's kin is one of the terrible things that it is always tragic to pursue. In that way, facing the tragic question reinforces moral commitments that should be reinforced, particularly in wartime.

But sometimes recognition of the losing claim has a more constructive function in long-term political planning. Consider Sophocles' *Antigone*.[18] Creon tells the entire city that anyone who offers burial to the traitor Polynices is a traitor to the city, and will be put to death. Antigone cannot accept the edict, because it asks her to violate a fundamental religious obligation to seek burial for her kin. As Hegel correctly argued, each protagonist is narrow, thinking only of one sphere of value and neglecting the claim of the other. Creon thinks only of the health of the city, neglecting the "unwritten laws" of family obligation. Antigone thinks only of the family, failing to recognize the crisis of the city. We may add that for this very reason each has an impoverished conception not only of value in general but also of his or her own cherished sphere of value. As Haemon points out, Creon fails to recognize that citizens are also members of families, and that

[17] Indeed, we might say that the main importance of reparations, too, is expressive. Obviously the fact that my grandmother-in-law received a regular income from the German government did nothing to bring back the family members who had perished during the Holocaust. Although the financial support was not negligible, its primary significance was as a public expression of wrongdoing and the determination to do things differently in the future.

[18] My interpretation is defended with a lot of textual detail and full discussion of the scholarly literature in *Fragility* chap. 3.

therefore a protector of the city who neglects these values is hardly protecting the city at all. Antigone fails to note that families also live in cities, which must survive if the survival of the family is to be ensured. A person who thought well about Antigone's choice would see that it is genuinely a tragedy: there is no "right answer," because both alternatives contain serious wrongdoing. Burying a traitor is a serious wrong to the city, but for Antigone not to bury him involves a serious religious violation. Because neither sees the tragedy inherent in the situation, because neither so much as poses the tragic question, both are in these two distinct ways impoverished political actors.

And this makes a huge difference for the political future. The drama depicts a very extreme situation, which is unlikely to occur often. In this extreme situation, where the city has been invaded by a member of its own ruling household, there may be no avoiding a tragic clash of duties. But a protagonist who faced the tragic question squarely would be prompted to have a group of highly useful thoughts about governance in general. In particular, noting that both the well-being of the city and the "unwritten laws" of religious obligation are of central ethical importance, he or she would be led to want a city that makes room for people to pursue their familial religious obligations without running afoul of civic ordinances.[19] In other words, he or she would want a city such as

---

[19] In *Fragility* I note that this interpretation is shared by a number of critics, including I. M. Linforth, "Antigone and Creon," *University of California Publications in Classical Philology* 15 (1961): 183–260, at 257; Matthew Santirocco, "Justice in Sophocles' *Antigone*," *Philosophy and Literature* 4 (1980): 180–98, at 182, 194; Charles Segal, *Tragedy and Civilization: An Interpretation of Sophocles* (Cambridge: Harvard University Press, 1981), 205. Linforth: "For all Athenians, the play offers a powerful warning to see to it that the laws they enact are not in conflict with the laws of the gods." Segal: "Through its choral song, the *polis* arrives at self-awareness of the tensions between which it exists. Embodying these tensions in art, it can confront them and work towards their mediation, even though mediation is not permitted to the tragic heroes within the spectacle itself. The play in its social and ritual contexts achieves for society what it refuses to the actors within its fiction. Its context affirms what its content denies."

Pericles claims to find in democratic Athens, when he boasts that public policy shows respect for unwritten law. Just as Americans believe that we can create a public order that builds in spaces for the free exercise of religion, in which individuals are not always tragically torn between civic ordinance and religious command, so ancient Athens had an analogous anti-tragic thought—as a direct result, quite possibly, of watching tragedies such as Sophocles' *Antigone*.

It was here, indeed, that Hegel found, plausibly, the political significance of tragedy. Tragedy reminds us of the deep importance of the spheres of life that are in conflict within the drama, and of the dire results when they are opposed and we have to choose between them. It therefore motivates us to imagine what a world would be like that did not confront people with such choices, a world of "concordant action" between the two spheres of value. In that sense, the end of the drama is written offstage, by citizens who enact these insights in their own constructive political reflection. "The true course of dramatic development consists in the annulment of *contradictions* viewed as such, in the reconciliation of the forces of human action, which alternately strive to negate each other in their conflict."[20]

Now, in one way Hegel's approach to tragedy is too simple. For it ignores the possibility that some degree of tragedy is a structural feature of human life.[21] Many distinct spheres of value claim our attention and commitment. As Greek polytheism expresses the insight, there are many gods, all of whom demand worship. But the gods do not agree. Therefore the contingencies

---

[20] Extract from *The Philosophy of Fine Art*, trans. P. B. Osmaston, vol. 4, reproduced in *Hegel on Tragedy*, ed. A. and H. Paolucci (New York: Dover, 1975), 68, 71.

[21] This was the emphasis of my reading of the *Antigone*; a similar view is defended in "Flawed Crystals," in *Love's Knowledge* (New York: Oxford University Press, 1990), where I call moral dilemmas a secular analogue of Original Sin: you can't live a fully pure life, a life in which you are false to no value.

of life make it almost inevitable that some disharmony will materialize among our many commitments. The only alternative to the permanent possibility of tragedy would appear to be a life so impoverished in value that it neglects many things that human beings should not neglect. And of course such a life does not really avoid tragedy: it just fails to see the tragedy involved in its own neglect of genuine values. Relations within the family—and between the family and the public sphere—are one area where we might expect a permanent possibility of tragedy, no matter how well we arrange things.[22]

In another way, however, Hegel gives us the best strategy to follow, especially in political life. In political life we frequently have to try to balance diverse goods that may come into conflict. Among these will be fundamental entitlements of citizens, such as those that are recognized in a list of basic constitutional rights. One good way of thinking about fundamental rights is that they are entitlements founded upon justice, such that it is always tragic, always a serious wrong, when a citizen is deprived of them. For that reason, it is very useful to consider apparently irresolvable tensions between two spheres of entitlement with Hegel's idea in view. For we really do not know whether a harmonious fostering of two apparently opposed values can be achieved—until we try to bring that about. Many people in many places have thought that a harmonious accommodation between religion and the state is just impossible. Athens tried to prove them wrong. Modern liberal states—grappling with the even thornier problem of the plurality of religions, and of secular views of the good—all in their own ways try to prove them wrong. To a great extent, a political regime like ours does enable citizens to avoid Antigone-like tragedies. That is what is meant by saying—as the Supreme Court said until the unfortunate decision in *Employment Division*

---

[22] See the similar argument in Marcus, "Moral Dilemmas and Consistency."

v. Smith,[23] and as Congress said in passing the Religious Freedom Restoration Act—that the state may not impose a "substantial burden" on an individual's free exercise of religion without a "compelling state interest."[24] Creon, presumably, had such an interest, and so too will quite a few other state actors. Consequently, there will be a residuum of tragedy left even in the Hegelian nation. But we proclaim that we do our best to keep tragedy at bay. We do so because we understand the force of the tragic question: understand, that is, that to require individuals to depart from their religious commitments is not just to impose an inconvenience, it is to ask something that goes to the heart of their being. It is to deprive them of a sphere of liberty to which, as citizens, they have an entitlement based upon justice.

Often we do not know what arrangements we are capable of making until we have faced the tragic question with Hegel's idea in mind. Consider one more example, a true modern story. Its content is more mundane than that of my mythic examples; in many ways, given that the harms done are smaller and possibly not irreparable, it will look less tragic. But it has a similar structure, and it raises similar Hegelian questions. Tragic cases, recall, are defined by the presence of serious wrongdoing on both sides; the wrongdoing does not always involve killing people; it may involve only neglect of some important obligation.

When I began teaching as an assistant professor at Harvard, my daughter was three years old. Because my husband taught in another city, I was in effect a single parent. I was lucky enough to be able to afford a first-rate child-care center, which offered a good environment for my daughter during usual working hours.

---

[23] This decision removed the requirement of "compelling state interest" when the religion's free exercise runs up against "laws of general applicability." At stake was the use of peyote in a sacred ceremony by Native Americans in the state of Oregon.

[24] For my own discussion of the cases, and a proposal based on the language of RFRA, see *Women and Human Development*, chap. 3.

On the other hand, my colleagues, oblivious to this situation, insisted on scheduling important meetings at night or, worse still, in the late afternoon and early evening, when my daughter would particularly need to have me there. Choices about what to do were one problem I had constantly. But I felt that I had another problem as well: for, often, neither of the alternatives looked morally acceptable. Either I would be deserting my duty to my colleagues or I would be deserting my duty to and love of my daughter. The tragic question kept rearing its head, and frequently its answer was "no."

Obviously enough, this string of minitragedies was the result of obtuseness. The arrangements my colleagues had made about colloquia were neither necessary nor sensible. Because it had never dawned on most of them to think that a person ought to be able to be both a good primary caretaking parent and a good colleague, they had never bothered to think what very simple changes in the daily arrangements might be made to remove the problem. Nobody could talk about this; nobody could draw attention to it. I recall the day when this changed. At an important lecture by a major visiting philosopher, held as usual at 5:00 and (implicitly) mandatory for junior faculty, we reached the question period (by now it's after 6:00—I've gotten a sitter to pick my daughter up from child care). Robert Nozick stood up and said, with the carefree subversiveness of which only the tenured are capable, "I have to go now: I have to pick up my son from hockey practice."

This was a moment of Hegelian *Aufhebung*: the first public acknowledgment that there was a tension between two spheres of value and that we had not been managing that tension very well. By coming out as a parent, Nozick had posed the tragic question to us all, challenging us to think better about it. It was unclear whether Nozick thought that his own case had the structure of a tragic dilemma: as a tenured person, and a remarkably independent one at that, he might not have thought he had any duty to attend the colloquium. But he drew attention to the predicament of others who were more vulnerable and who had similar family obligations.[25]

How are such cases connected with the diversity of goods? In, I think, the following way. If one saw every such conflict as containing simply different quantities of the very same homogeneous value-stuff, then it would not be so morally grave that only one can be chosen. If the choice to go to that department meeting instead of seeing my daughter perform were just like having $200 instead of having $50, then it does not appear that a distinctive claim is being neglected. But because the good, including the morally good, is heterogeneous and there are distinctive potentially conflicting claims, because my daughter is not just a little piece of my professional life but a distinct person with her own distinctive claims, such conflicts have a residuum of unsatisfied obligation. In that sense, Utilitarianism is the anti-tragic philosophy par excellence.[26]

Thomson's treatment of "ought" appears to me to lack the recognition of tragedy, and thus it appears to lack an important feature. She moves straight from the prima facie conflict of oughts to an all-things-considered ought, with no sense that there might remain another genuine "ought" on the scene whose demands have not been satisfied. Indeed, the rejection of the significance of tragedy is deeply built into her treatment of rights as well: in cases

---

[25] Later, he also made a formal protest against the nighttime seminar that was (again implicitly) mandatory for junior faculty, pointing out that it was a hardship for those who had children. He didn't succeed—the response was simply to say, of course it's not mandatory, but of course it was, and remained so. But the intervention showed that his remark about hockey was no chance matter.

[26] But of course many deontological views also duck the recognition of tragedy. Among them is, famously, Kant's view, which holds that there can be no genuine conflicts of duty. I have discussed this view extensively in *Fragility*, chap. 2. I believe that Kant ends up in this unsatisfactory position because he is reluctant to say that an accident in the world of nature could ever put an agent in a position in which he must violate a genuine duty.

where two rights-claims conflict, she holds that one is always overridden by the other, except in cases where there is a genuine tie. In those cases, Thomson holds, there are indeed two non-overridden rights, but this is not "theoretically interesting," because once we adopt some suitable decision procedure—for example, flipping a coin—"then presumably the winner, and only the winner, has a non-overridden right."

When Thomson arrives at her analysis of putative conflicts of justice with miserliness, or justice with justice, once again, she defines terms in such a way that the tragic conflict is removed. "It cannot be the case both that Alfred's *V*-ing is unjust and that his not *V*-ing is miserly." There is no inconsistency or oversight in Thomson's account: the way she has defined her terms, her assertion that there is no such conflict is perfectly correct. What I am saying, however, is that there is a human phenomenon of grave personal and political significance that is effaced from view by this way of putting things.

By effacing the phenomenon of tragedy, Thomson draws close to contemporary Utilitarian cost-benefit analysis, which asks what we ought to do by looking at our options, and ranking them by some procedure. Some forms of cost-benefit analysis assume the homogeneity of good, but many make no such commitment. Some are so vague and undertheorized that they do not make any theoretical claims that Thomson could find objectionable. What they share with her view is the emphasis on the fact that once we've found a suitable decision procedure, that's the end of the matter. The losing claim ceases to exert any pull.[27]

It seems to me that putting things this way is a big mistake in any view, but particularly in one that aims at including public

---

[27] I have discussed this issue extensively in "The Costs of Tragedy." For other critical discussions of cost-benefit analysis, see the excellent papers by Amartya Sen, by Henry Richardson, and by Matthew Adler and Eric Posner in the same issue of the *Journal of Legal Studies*.

choice within its domain. Let us imagine that a state commits itself, in its constitution, to an account of the basic entitlements of citizens. Now a situation comes along where it appears that these entitlements cannot all be made good: we have to choose. For example, to return to the *Antigone*, somebody's freedom of religion requires someone else to pay a high price in terms of liberty, or civic order, or whatever. Now, it seems to me that the analysis of what's to be done is an important part of the matter. And it is important in more than one way: not only in deciding what's to be done, but also in fixing the right level of entitlements themselves. For we do not want to live with tragedy all the time, and so we will sensibly prefer an account of religious free exercise (for example) that does not generate ubiquitous conflicts with other basic entitlements. To that extent I am in agreement with the Thomson strategy of defining the virtues in part by reference to situations of alleged or potential conflict.

But we should not go all the way with this strategy, for the reasons given by Hegel. Often, what generates the conflict is not any inherent intractability in the material of life; it is just human greed and laziness. My colleagues at Harvard might have concluded that changing the time of the colloquium was unnatural and impossible. That, indeed, is how people are inclined to view many irritating changes in their habits. As recently as 1873, the U.S. Supreme Court held that to allow women to be lawyers would go against "the nature of things."[28] Knowing that we are not reliable judges of the meaning of change for the overall order of society, we should not hold fundamental entitlements hostage to current social possibilities. We should be skeptical of claims that the costs of securing an important entitlement to all citizens will be prohibitive. Let's try first, we should say, and see how things go. And we should also be prepared to recognize that some

[28] *Bradwell v. Illinois*, 83 U.S. (16 Wall.) 130 (1873).

very important social goods, which should remain on the list of central entitlements, are not available, or not available without prohibitive costs, in our current social environment. This gives us a motivation to design things better, so that we will be able to secure the entitlement to people at some future time. Setting the level too low, in response to current possibilities and impossibilities, may be a recipe for social lassitude.

Consider the case of compulsory education in India. All Indian states require primary education; in many cases, secondary education is compulsory as well. But literacy rates remain low: about 35 percent for women, 65 percent for men in the nation as a whole. Economic necessity is clearly involved in this distressing pattern: poor parents need to rely on the labor of their children, whether in the home or outside it. Many families would be at risk of going under completely if they were to send all their children to government schools. And yet there are also signs that intelligent planning can make a difference. The state of Kerala, a relatively poor state, has an adolescent literacy rate of 99 percent for both boys and girls. The difference has a great deal to do with state policies: aggressive campaigning in favor of literacy; incentives to poor parents, in the form of a nutritious school lunch that goes some way to offsetting the losses to parents in child labor; and flexible multisession school hours.[29] If we look to states where literacy is particularly low, we find, correspondingly, an absence of intelligent planning. In some rural areas (in Andhra Pradesh, for example), there aren't any schools or teachers, since state gov-

[29] See Jean Drèze and Amartya Sen, *India: Economic Development and Social Opportunity* (Delhi: Oxford University Press, 1995). Kerala's relative poverty, Drèze and Sen argue, is due to its bad economic policies: permitting unions to drive wages up very high has caused employment to shift to neighboring states. On the other hand, health and education have been well promoted in the absence of robust economic growth. (They use this example, among others, to illustrate the fact that even in the absence of economic growth, one may achieve progress in these areas; on the other side, focusing only on economic growth—as other states have done—does not achieve progress in these areas.)

ernment is corrupt and inefficient and has not bothered to make things happen. In many others areas, government schools fail to offer flexible hours that make schooling possible for working children; Nongovernmental Organizations sometimes fill the gap, but sometimes they don't.

All this suggests that there is some point to setting a high threshold with regard to education, in a way that gives education the moral force of a basic entitlement—even if the level set cannot currently be achieved in many areas. This is in fact what India is now doing: a proposal to amend the Constitution's list of fundamental rights to include a fundamental right of primary and secondary education has recently been incorporated into the Constitution.[30] Obviously enough, amending the constitution does not all by itself change the conditions I have described. But it does give education a new moral and legal emphasis: it is now a fundamental entitlement of all citizens, the deprivation of which constitutes a tragic cost. It will also be possible to litigate against states or other public actors that deprive children of this fundamental right through deficient planning. Raising the tragic question gives a new urgency to political planning.

For these reasons, I believe that Thomson should be more willing than she is to admit the significance, indeed the salience, of conflicts between one right and another right, between justice and miserliness, between one instance of justice and another. The account thus becomes more complicated. But it seems to me to answer better, in this form, to the complexities of life.

[30] See Archana Mehendale, "Compulsory Primary Education in India: The Legal Framework," *From the Lawyers' Collective* 13 (April 1998): 4–12.

COMMENT

J. B. Schneewind

In Part I Judith Thomson argued against Utilitarianism and the general form of theory that it exemplifies, Consequentialism. These ethical theories assert that what makes an act the one you ought to do is its being the act whose consequences will contain more good, on balance, than any other act you could do. The simplest version holds that what makes an event or state of affairs good is its being pleasant. Thomson asserted that this claim is false, because not every pleasure is good: consider, for instance, the case of someone being pleased about another's suffering. The Consequentialist can fall back on a purely formal theory, holding that we ought to do what brings about more good events than any other act we can do. Thomson then argued that events, just as such, can't be good or bad. Aristotle objected to Plato's view of the good by saying that "good" is not univocal, because the criteria for being good differ from category to category. Similarly, Thomson claimed that when we call something good we are saying that it is good in some special way, as a hammer is good for nailing or hot lemonade good for soothing a sore throat. It makes no more sense to ask if an event is good or bad than it does to ask if a rock is good or bad. This seems to show that there is an unbridgeable gap between the facts about events and values. But in particular cases, we know perfectly well how to tell whether a thing of a specific kind is good or not, or is good for someone or not. This is true even though there is no single principle that enables us to infer the goodness from the facts. And when we know that doing something would be good in some way, we have a reason for doing it. The question that remains is this: which of the acts that we have a reason to do are the acts we ought to do? Before turning to answer this question Thomson provides a sketch of what it is to have a reason, but I shall not try to summarize her view.

In Part II Thomson sketches her answer to the question about what we ought to do. Her aim is not to provide a full theory. It is rather to show what the "structure" of such a theory must be. With the Consequentialist she thinks that it is the goodness of what we do or bring about that makes an act obligatory. But although all goods are "good in a way," it does not follow that all oughts are "ought in a way." We can ask for and give decisive advice about what someone ought to do. We can do so because we can compare different sorts of good and tell which is most important, or carries most weight. Practical reasoning, Thomson thinks, is just comparing goods and ills in this way in order to determine what we ought to do. But against Consequentialism Thomson holds that these comparisons do not invoke a common measuring stick. Although we rank possible good outcomes of acts as more or less weighty, or important, we have no single ranking or principle that covers all sets of outcomes.

Some acts affect only the person acting. In such a case, once the agent knows how to get a good for himself that isn't outweighed by any ills, he knows what he ought to do. The knowledge of the weighted goods and ills by itself directly entails the "ought" conclusion. And once we understand how these single-person goods work, we can understand moral goods and ills. Morality enters when we consider the nonmoral goods and ills that result for everyone affected by an act. We are morally good or bad by being just or unjust, generous or miserly, in distributing these goods and ills. If some possible act would be unjust or miserly, this directly entails that we ought not to do it. No rule or principle has to be given to license the inference from "This act would be unjust" to "I ought not to do this act." Finally, Thomson argues, although we ought never to be unjust or miserly, we need not do every just act or every generous act.

Thomson gives examples in which she says that it is "intuitively plain" (I.16) that some good, such as saving a human life, is vastly more important than another, say soothing a sore throat. She does not try to explain our ability to make these comparisons, nor does she attempt to justify the epistemic status she assigns to our intuitions. Her invocations of practical reason and her examples suggest that she takes moral theory to be concerned with how we must think when we ask what we ought to do next. Her idea seems to be that we can get on with answering questions of that kind without troubling about how we know. If we have a mistaken moral theory, however, we may make mistaken moral judgements, or find ourselves in insoluble quandaries because we are asking the wrong question. Perhaps avoiding these errors is the benefit she expects from having the right ethical theory.

Disagreement provides the philosopher's equivalent of the scientist's laboratory. But I find much that Thomson says quite convincing. Rather than question particular points, I shall raise a general issue about the nature of her enterprise. I shall do so by noting one central way in which her view about "ought" differs from one of the main earlier views of it.

Thomson labels the sense of "ought" with which she is concerned the "advice" sense. This is a misleading label. If by way of offering you some advice I tell you that you ought to sell those shares now, you can take my advice or leave it: it's your business. But Thomson is not restricting herself to this sort of "ought" or to "ought" used to give this sort of directive. Her account is

meant to cover the use of "ought" with which we express the belief that there is something that you have to do, like it or not, and
that your doing so is other people's business, not just yours. The
structure of the theory she gives ties claims about what someone
ought to do directly to claims about good or about rights. Certain
claims about one or the other lead immediately to conclusions
about what someone ought to do. It is a simple structure.

In the seventeenth century modern natural law theorists explained the notion of "ought" by saying that it is morally necessary for you to do what you ought to do in this sense. They then
explained moral necessity as being constituted by a law that requires agents to do acts of a specified kind. A law presupposes a
lawgiver who has the proper authority over his subjects. And a
lawgiver, by definition, must have the power to punish disobe-
dience. The magistrate creates political oughts for his subjects
but not for those under other jurisdictions. The distinctively
moral ought arises, these thinkers held, when God lays down laws
for all human beings. But the general structure of a theory about
"ought" involves more than Thomson's structure does. The natural lawyers distinguished giving advice from obligating as two
different kinds of activity in which words like "ought" might be
used. Obligating someone to do something is not leaving it up to
his good pleasure to do or not to do, while advising someone
leaves it up to him to do or not.

Most of the natural law theorists would have agreed with
Thomson about what she calls the "second-order" feature of
morality—that the moral ought presupposes some nonmoral or
natural goods and ills and directs the ways we are to produce and
distribute these. But they would have rejected her claim that
knowledge of these natural goods and ills entails, all by itself,
conclusions about what we ought to do. They would have pointed
out that Thomson has accepted a main claim made by Leibniz,
who was a Consequentialist theorist. On his view, our awareness

129

that an act will bring about the greatest increase in good is, by itself, what makes it morally necessary for us to do that act. He thinks that no rule or principle is needed to license the move from "is good" to "ought"; and Thomson agrees with this part of his view. The natural lawyers would have thought that Thomson and Leibniz both miss the central point about the moral "ought"— that it shows our subjection to a divine ruler to whom we owe obedience. The lawyers would have added another point. When you do something because you are required to do it, they held, you act from a motive that is different from the motive you have when you do something because you want to. But you act as you want to when you do something because you think it would bring about good. And this blurs the line between the ought of advice and the moral ought. We need a divinely given law, so these theorists would have said, to bridge the gap between "is naturally good" and "ought to do" and also to show how God is essential to morality and to our lives.

The "ought" that Thomson is discussing plays the same role in morality as the "ought" that the natural lawyers had in view. So I do not think that she is explaining a different concept or a different sense of "ought." What are we to make, then, of the differences between the natural law account and Thomson's account? Thomson presents her explanations, in both Parts, as if they concerned concepts that are beyond time. The Greeks understood geometrical concepts just as we do, she might say, and it is no different with moral concepts. After all, Aristotle spoke of how the sense of "good" varies from kind of thing to kind of thing, much as Thomson does. But I think it is not so simple. Thomson gives a brilliant account of how we understand the central moral concept "ought," but the "we" here is not the whole human race. It is those of us who, in the last couple of centuries, have wholly detached morality from religion and from external authority. The structure of the theory of "ought" that she presents is the structure of a morality that has come to be available in our culture. It may not, even now, be the only one that people accept.

Other concepts central to morality have also changed, in related ways. In his elegant book *The Moral Problem*, Michael Smith says that anyone who understands our moral language will take it to be a platitudinous truth that moral knowledge is equally available to every normal adult.[1] But in the seventeenth and eighteenth centuries this was far from being taken as an incontestable and trivial truth. It was taken to be plainly false. The common belief was that those who are better educated, or cleverer, or more blessed by God's grace must be moral authorities for all the rest—for the majority, and especially women and the lower orders. Smith's account may be correct as regards the way we now understand the availability of moral knowledge. Perhaps this understanding is built into our moral concepts or moral vocabulary, as he thinks. But if so, our present understanding reflects a major change from an earlier estimate of the capacities of ordinary people. And the change is essentially a *moral* change. We now think that we ought to treat everyone, regardless of their education or class, as being as capable as we are of entering into moral discussion. Perhaps, as Smith claims, this belief is now built into our moral concepts. But it was not always so.

Thomson's thesis about the entailment relations between goods and oughts is thus more than a thesis about the relations of central moral concepts, and more than a logical thesis about the so-called is-ought gap. It carries a specific way of understanding the mode of self-direction that we take to be central to morality. I suspect that most of us share this view of morality; and it is no deprecation of it to see it as a historical achievement. Thomson's lectures help us toward an understanding of beliefs that are ours, although they have not always been everyone's.

[1] Michael Smith, *The Moral Problem* (London: Basil Blackwell, 1994), 5.

COMMENT

Barbara Herrnstein Smith

JUDITH THOMSON sees us as inhabiting a culture of "deep [moral] skepticism," one sign of which is the reluctance of her freshmen students to declare that their moral convictions are objectively true. She grants that this skepticism does not have any noticeable practical effects (it does not deter those freshmen or most other people from having moral convictions or acting upon them), but she thinks there is, philosophically speaking, something disturbing about this situation. Accordingly, she has gone to some trouble here to demonstrate that, contrary to the idea of a fact-value gap, we can and do reason from facts to objectively true judgments: clearly so in the case of judgments of practical and aesthetic goodness, she maintains, but equally so in the case of judgments of moral goodness—though we might, she suggests, do the latter reasoning better if we had on hand the sort of moral theory she outlines here, or at least be better able to refute skepticism as to its possibility.

"Goodness and Advice" exhibits many of the features that count as rigor in contemporary academic-philosophic circles, and some of Professor Thomson's substantive observations, especially those regarding the *tacit* specifications commonly attached to value-judgments, are, in my view, worth stressing in value-theory. At the same time, however, the conceptual and pragmatic value of her arguments and proposals appears limited by their reliance on a set of assumptions, claims, and procedures that, though standard in much contemporary moral philosophy, could also be seen as exceedingly confined. The confinements here may be the source of the rigor just noted; the limited conceptual and pragmatic value may be its price.

1.

My comments are in four parts, beginning here with some observations on Thomson's conception of value-judgments and, relatedly, on her interpretation of the fact-value gap.

Thomson deplores the doctrine of a fact-value gap because it implies, falsely she believes, that nobody can say of some value-judgment that *it is true*. It is important, she believes, that we be able to say that because, as she sees it, the only alternative would be to accept the idea that value-ascriptions are mere expressions of tastes or attitudes and thus, presumably, though she does not make the point explicitly, worth very little. There are, however, other alternatives. For example, one may view such ascriptions—that is, overt statements of the goodness or badness, rightness or wrongness, beauty or ugliness (and so forth) of acts or objects—as neither fundamentally true/false propositions nor ("mere") subjective expressions, but, rather, as forms of social communication, which, like all other verbal utterances, have a wide range of de-sired/able functions that may be performed better or worse, as assessed from various perspectives. Under such an alternative view, the formal features of a particular value-judgment—that is, how it is framed verbally, including its syntax, modality, diction, and other communicative features (for example, whether it is of-fered as a simple unqualified statement, such as "Two thumbs up!" or "Gorgeous hat!" or as a more elaborated and highly qual-ified statement, such as "A vile way, in my opinion, to behave to-ward a student")—would be seen as shaped by various contingent conditions, including the circumstantial context of its utterance, the relation of the speaker to his or her audience, and various relevant interests and beliefs, often tacit, that may or may not be shared between them. Also accordingly, the *value* of a particular value-judgment (or, as Thomson might put it, its *goodness-in-a-way*)—including the value of its expression, as is likely to be the case, of certain tastes or attitudes, whether idiosyncratic or more or less widely shared among the members of some relevant community—would be measurable by parameters other than, in the classic sense, truth-value: for example, by its communicative force, social effectivity, or informativeness for the particular audience to whom it is addressed and/or for various other people who may otherwise encounter it. These alternative measures of value, being circumstantially contingent and subject-variable, are not, of course, objective in the technical sense. But, clearly, neither are they negligible—except, as it appears, from the perspective of a strenuously confined notion of the nature and operations of such judgments.[1]

As commonly explained, the central theoretical problem involved in the idea of a fact-value gap is that because of a difference in logical kinds between (a) empirical descriptions or factual statements and (b) value-judgments or normative statements, one cannot deduce (or, in Thomson's idiom, "reason to") the latter from the former. As it is sometimes put, though you can get from one "is" to another "is," for example, from a general empirical law to a particular empirical fact, or from one "ought" to another "ought," for example, from a general normative statement to a particular moral judgment, you cannot extract an "ought," that is, a putatively objective moral directive, from an "is," that is, the

---

[1] For further discussion of these points, see Barbara Herrnstein Smith, *Contingencies of Value: Alternative Perspectives for Critical Theory* (Cambridge: Harvard University Press, 1988).

statement of an empirical state of affairs, however general, extensive, or well validated. It is also often observed that claims to have
done so—that is, to have derived an "ought" from an "is"—
usually involve the smuggling in of some other taken-for-granted
norm or judgment that is itself ungrounded. The fact-value gap is
usually invoked to rebut the claim that some alleged moral requirement (for example, incest avoidance, premarital chastity, or
the equal distribution of goods) is validated by this or that scien-
tific finding or based on the laws of nature or of history. It is not
commonly invoked to rebut the claim, which seems to be Thomson's main concern here, that moral judgments can be true. In
any case, it is not clear that her line of counterargument here
engages the theoretical difficulty indicated above. Rather, she appears recurrently to finesse it via the creation and deployment of
a curiously hybrid sort of statement that she calls an "evaluative
or normative fact" (for example, "it is wrong to infringe other
people's rights"), which is said to mediate logically between some
supposedly clearly factual statement about a proposed act (for example, "A's breaking his promise would infringe B's rights") and
a proper moral judgment of that act (for example, here, "A ought
not to break his promise). The trouble with this hopeful fact-
value bridge is not only that so many of the supposed facts are
themselves normative and thus already on the value side of the
gap, but that they are truisms, self-evident because little more
than a rearrangement of conventional definitions. Accordingly,
the value-judgements derived from them, though logically
proper, are little more than tautologies. I'll return to this point.

2.

My second comment—or, here, question—concerns the logical/
cognitive operation of the hypothetical cases that Thomson devises both to exemplify the types of reasoning she proposes and
also to demonstrate their intuitive rightness or plausibility. The

question is highlighted by the egregious, though certainly determined, spareness and triviality of many of these examples and, likewise, of the prudential or moral options they present: for example, whether or not to drink a glass of hot lemonade, ring a doorbell, and so forth. The idea, presumably, is that, where a hypothetical is so trifling that no one could have any conceivable interest much less prior individual convictions or biases with respect to its specific substantive features, the focus of attention can fall squarely, purely, and properly on its abstract—and thus more broadly generalizable—formal or logical features.

The question, however, is whether, in presenting such severely stripped-down examples and banishing virtually all sources of substantive interest in a situation or its outcome, Thomson has not also eliminated an inevitable and indeed crucially motivating element of the processes of assessment performed by sublunary beings. Indeed, one may ask whether the intuitive rightness of the judgments and principles thereby illustrated or tested, and the presumed objectivity and generality of application thereby secured for them, may not be spurious—artifacts of the quite specific but arguably artificial and irrelevant ways in which those judgments and principles have been generated and validated. A related question here and in all case-based moral theory is how drastically, in claiming to derive general moral rules by expansion or analogy from particular "clear-to-everyone" cases, we can or should abstract away from the specific features of those cases, and whether, in so abstracting, we may not lose precisely what makes one or another judgment about them appear so intuitively plain: that is, the vividness, detail, and evocativeness (such as they may be) of their specific, not generic, features.

Either way, what gets slighted is the significance, in the actual *processes* of our evaluative activities, of our ongoing responsiveness to a wide range of specific but contingent factors, not all of which could be explicitly charted or formally articulated, much less de-

scribed in general terms: for example, what we know or can sur-
mise of the specific, perhaps highly individual, temperaments, re-
sources, prior experiences, or current expectations of various persons affected by our actions; what we can imagine, even if not
confidently predict, as the longer-range and more diffuse effects
of our acts (or, better, *courses* of action), including their effects on
particular but nonindividual aspects of our worlds, such as com-
munities, institutions, or practices; and, hardly to be omitted
here, the particular sense of responsibility or concern we may feel
for the welfare of certain persons or aspects of the world by virtue
of their familial, institutional, personal-historical, or other relation to us. It might be replied that personal, highly individuated
considerations of the latter kinds are *properly* slighted in arriving
at moral judgments because they compromise the objectivity of
such judgments and thus keep them from being genuinely moral
and possibly true. But this reply simply affirms the particular,
dubiously privileged definition of moral judgment assumed in
Thomson's lectures, and thus begs the fundamental question at
issue here.

I stress *processes* of evaluative activity and *courses* of action above
as preferable to the static and atomistic conception of judgments
and acts that appears also to be assumed in Thomson's lectures: a
conception of them, that is, as clearly bounded, mutually separa-
ble, individually discrete, and temporally sequential. In the alternative conception signaled above, our judgments, actions, and the
relations between them would be seen as more fluid, dynamic,
and reciprocally interactive than conventionally represented in
moral philosophy. Accordingly, it could be thought that what
makes a particular process-of-evaluation/course-of-action ethically estimable is not the precision of the evaluator/agent's prior
calculations of the relative harms and benefits of some discrete act
to some specific set of beings or the putative objective truth of the
moral principles to which those calculations are referred, but,

rather, the range, subtlety, and pertinence of the conditions to which it is responsive and the fineness of its continuously adjusted attunement to its own observed and imagined effects. So understood, the process of ethically responsible evaluation-action would be, in effect, coextensive with, and in some senses indistinguishable from, the conduct of the evaluator-agent's life. Such an idea of the ethical is no doubt consonant along many lines with Thomson's views of the moral worthiness of acts and the propriety of moral judgments. The quality of ongoing, dynamic responsiveness stressed here, however, is not captured by the more abstract, bounded, and linear sequences of moral reasoning that she offers as models; nor could it be captured, I think, by any system of moral principles or method of moral deduction as such.

3.

We can and do reason, Thomson insists, from facts to true moral judgments. For example, from the facts (a) that one ought not to act unjustly, (b) that it is unjust to infringe on someone's rights, (c) that breaking a promise infringes on a person's right to expect that a promise will be kept, and (d) that in not returning the five dollars he promised to repay Bertha, Albert would be breaking his promise to her, one (anyone) can reason to the objectively true moral judgment, "Albert *ought to* pay the five dollars back to Bertha." All this seems very clear, coherent, and logical. The question is *why*.

The answer, I would suggest, is that the "facts" deployed in this and similar chains of reasoning are true only by virtue of a system of prior interlocked definition: that is, standard verbal usages and formal philosophical definitions of terms such as "just," "unjust," "rights," "promises," "ought to," "moral," and so forth, such that the syntactic-conceptual-pragmatic operations of each are shaped by and depend on the operations of one or more of the others. What is significant here is that the interlocking takes place not in an abstract, disembodied realm of putatively objective moral facts and purely logical relations, but in the actual verbal and intellectual practices and experiences of the members of a particular community. The latter are "us," both (a) the sorts of educated, literate people whose current usages of the terms in question, and whose confident current intuitions about the propriety of various statements applying them to various situations, Thomson invokes as pointing to and validating the moral principles and judgments she endorses here, *and also* (b) her audiences: that is, the sorts of educated, literate people—including, of course, other moral philosophers—who attend or read her lectures and to whom she evidently hopes and expects these normative facts, chains of reasoning, and moral judgments to appear clear, logically coherent, and true. Indeed, in view of the identity of these two populations, it is not surprising that there is so much convergence in "our" intuitions of rightness or wrongness, consistency or inconsistency, plausibility or implausibility, manifest plainness or ambiguity (and so forth) with respect to the application of those terms in the sorts of hypothetical statements and situations she devises. Not surprising but also not especially informative. For this convergence attests not, as Thomson seems to believe, to the inherent, objective, and presumptively universal (im)propriety, necessity, optionality, and/or truth of the acts, principles, and judgments in question but, rather, to the similarity of certain learned practices and recurrent experiences among the members of a particular community ("us"). I am not suggesting that this system of learned relations is purely interlinguistic—that is, without any practical efficacy—or unique to the members of a particular community. I am suggesting, however, that it is generated and sustained by social-pragmatic and cognitive dynamics (which, as such, may be widespread and lead to relatively durable effects) rather than by universal moral intuitions or purely logical relations among autonomous concepts.

Thomson is herself extensively concerned with common verbal usage and recommends that it be closely attended by moral philosophers. For example, she writes: "The adjective 'good' is among the most commonly used in the English language. What we should have been doing is to look at how it is in fact used, and at what it does in fact settle that it is or is not applicable" (I.8). Similarly, later, norms of verbal usage and/or shared intuitions about the plausibility of the application of certain terms are her warrant for claiming that "reasons" must be "facts" (I.9), that only "objective" ways of "being good or bad" count as "moral" (I.11), that these ways cannot be the sort that depend on an agent's "subjective state of mind" (II.5), and that this explains why an act's being "just" or "unjust" *is* an "objective" matter while its being "morally good" or "morally bad" is *not* (II.6). Again, however, and contrary to what Professor Thomson seems to believe, what these verbal usages and shared intuitions reveal is not the objective moral status of the hypothetical acts or judgments to which they are applied but, rather, prevailing communal norms of verbal practice and conduct: that is, current standards of verbal propriety and official/public ideas about proper ways of acting. What Thomson has done here is uncovered a good number of such norms, articulated them formally as moral principles, and organized them in accord with academic-philosophical standards of clarity, rigor, and coherence. All of these are no doubt worthy or at least valued philosophical activities but, given the understanding of them just suggested, it appears that the authority and force of such principles, their power to compel action or belief, can be no greater or indeed *other* than the social and cognitive power—hardly, of course, to be underestimated—of the communal norms and beliefs they recapitulate.

Evidently a good many people are inclined to believe and to say, when asked by someone, including themselves in the role of moral philosopher, that it's right to do what one ought to, that one ought not to do what's unjust, that it's morally good but not required to do what is generous, and that acting ungenerously is not morally wrong but certainly not what one ought to do. All these statements are, as Thomson claims, true normative facts, but only in that they are truisms, which is to say that the affirmation of their truth consists only of underlining rhetorically the fact that a good many people are inclined to believe and say such things. Moral theory, practiced this way, can tell us what ideas of proper moral conduct currently prevail in our community and how those ideas can be connected with maximal internal coherence. It can also tell us what we *believe* are good and better reasons for action. It cannot tell us, however, which acts or reasons are objectively good or objectively better than others. Nor is it clear that the idea of objective goodness, with respect to acts, reasons, judgments, or anything else, makes any sense.

Which brings me to my fourth and final set of comments.

4.

In Part I, Thomson argues vigorously against the idea—crucial, she remarks, to a number of dominant moral theories—that goodness is a simple property or parameter. When people say that something is good, she observes, what they mean, even though they may not make these specifications explicit, is that it is good *in some way*, *as some kind of thing*, *for some use*, and/or *for someone*. All this seems to me to move in a desirable direction for a theory of value judgments. At the same time, however, the alternative conception of goodness that Thomson develops in Part II remains limited, in my view, insofar as it ignores certain other specifications, arguably no less significant, that could also be seen as implied—if not stated explicitly—when we speak of a thing as *good*: notably, good *under some more or less specific set of conditions* and good *from the perspective of some more or less specific set of subjects*.

It may be that Thomson has not noticed these other implicit specifications or that she has noticed but rejected them as having too strong a whiff of Demon Relativism about them: certainly they pose problems for the classic idea that some kinds of goodness are unconditional and transpersonal, and for the related idea that some judgments of value are unconditionally and objectively true.

The latter suspicion is reinforced by Thomson's invocation, in regard to what she characterizes as the "messiness" of tastes, of the classic distinction between, as it is commonly put, mere statements of personal preference and genuine judgments of value: that is, between, on the one hand, statements such as "I (or they) like it" and, on the other hand, statements such as "It is beautiful" or "It is good" or, as in the example of the distinction she presents, "It is not good[-tasting]." "Lots of people," Thomson observes, "like the taste of strawberry Kool-Aid: it sells very well indeed." "For all that," she continues, "strawberry Kool-Aid does not taste good" (I.8). This is, to my ears, a very peculiar-sounding sequence of statements—unless I assume that when she says "strawberry Kool-Aid does not taste good," what Thomson means is that it does not or would not taste good *to the members of some implied but more or less specific population of subjects*: presumably, here, people like herself and most of the members of her immediate audience with what we call sophisticated tastes, as distinct from young children or people such as some of my North Carolina neighbors with an innate or culturally induced sweet tooth (she should taste those peach cobblers!).

I am not suggesting that Thomson's distinction between something's being liked by many people and its being good (or bad) is elitist. The same type of distinction is exhibited in the local teenager's remark to his friends, "Oh, yeah, my mom and all my aunts and sisters loved that tear-jerker at the Chelsea, but it's the pits." I would suggest, however, that, in framing the distinction, she, like the teenager, tacitly privileges the preferences or tastes of a more or less specific population of subjects as normative for the determination of goodness in that respect. Such tacit privileging of the tastes or perspectives of particular sets of subjects is, I believe, a common feature of all value ascriptions, moral, aesthetic and other, and is not itself ethically or otherwise objectionable. Nor does it, I think, compromise the communicative value of such judgments along the lines discussed in section 1 above. On the contrary, the *specificity* of the implied set of subjects (sophisticated urbanites versus children and country people, male adolescents versus women, and so forth), along with other—also often tacit—specifications that Thomson indicates (for example, good in *this* way rather than *that* way—and, I would add, good under *these* rather than *those* conditions of encounter), is, I believe, a significant part of what gives those judgments their interest, informativeness, and appropriability to those to whom they are addressed and, duly interpreted, to various other audiences.[2] Problems and objections flow not from the privileging as such but, rather, from its *denial*, as in claims made for the objectivity, unconditionality, and/or universal validity of such arguably (in that case) peremptory judgments. The local teenager in my example would probably be reluctant to press claims of that sort for his film assessments or, indeed, might regard such objectivist, universalist claims as, intuitively, somehow off base—which would put him, of course, in the company of Thomson's freshmen philosophy students, whose comparable reluctances or refusals are, for her, signs of the deep moral skepticism currently rampant among members of the literate middle classes.

---

[2] In interpreting overt value-ascriptions, listeners and readers usually assume that certain specifications and/or normative conditions are implied, if not explicitly stated, and can also usually infer them more or less accurately from the context, as one imagines would happen in the case of the teenager's brief but conceivably highly informative movie review.

Thomson explains the "messiness" of determinations of aesthetic goodness as due in part to our lack of proper "phenomenological characterizations of tastes." "Most of us" she observes, "do not really attend to tastes very closely, and do not notice in them what a professional notices." What she seems to have in mind here as lacking is something like a catalog of normative facts of taste that would bridge the aesthetic fact-value gap by permitting us to reason from the putatively objectively determinable features of objects—such as, perhaps, the chemical composition of strawberry Kool-Aid or, in her related example, what an attentive professional determines as the "austerity" and "delicacy" of the taste of a certain brand of brandy—to true judgments of their objective good-tastingness. If so, then I would say that, in view of the long history and unqualified failure of efforts to develop such an objectivist aesthetics in the past, the prospects for a successful one emerging in the future appear pretty slim. The fundamental question raised by her lectures, of course, is whether the prospects are any better for the sort of objectivist moral theory she outlines here.

This last question suggests that the skepticism Thomson associates with a reluctance to make objectivist claims for value-judgments, and which, taken as a sign of incipient moral lassitude or at least *moral-theory* lassitude, she may seek to overcome in her freshmen students, might be better understood as a duly critical stance toward some of the classic assumptions, claims, and procedures of moral philosophy and, as such, fostered, where it occurs, as a hopeful sign of intellectual vitality.

Reply to Commentators

REPLY TO COMMENTATORS

Judith Jarvis Thomson

I AM GRATEFUL to the commentators for the attention they paid to the material in Parts I and II, and for the criticisms they made of it. I haven't space to reply to all of their objections; I will try to reply to those that seem to me to be most important to them.

1. *Method*

Barbara Herrnstein Smith and Philip Fisher object to the hypothetical cases I focus on. I ask whether Alfred ought to press a certain doorbell, whether a person ought to drink some hot lemonade, and so on. Herrnstein Smith calls them trivial. Well, they might or might not be trivial. It might matter greatly whether a person presses a doorbell or drinks some hot lemonade; you would have to hear more about the agents and their circumstances to find out whether or not it matters whether they do.

Perhaps Alfred ought to press the doorbell, perhaps it is not the case that he ought to. What concerns me is the question what would make it the case that he ought to. What do we have to find out if we are to find out whether he ought to? That is what a moral theory should tell us.

Fisher objects that there are better "entry points" into ethics than "isolated, free standing, one-time events—like Alfred at the doorbell . . ." I am not entirely clear what troubles him. Is it the case that Marvin ought to break Muriel's arm? One hopes that Marvin's breaking Muriel's arm would also be a one-time event. (Though perhaps Herrnstein Smith would say that it is not trivial whether Marvin does this.) And would Fisher therefore say that this event too would be a bad entry point into ethics?

Such hypothetical cases as I invite attention to can be used to play a number of different roles in moral theory. Alfred appeared in Part I in the following way. I had wanted to bring out why a person might be tempted to opt for Consequentialism—which says that a person ought to do a thing if and only if the world will be better if he does it than if he does any of the other things it is open to him to do at the time. The literature of moral theory is full of rebuttals of Consequentialism; we do well to try to be clear first, however, why a person might think it a plausible idea. Very well, consider Alfred, who is standing in a certain doorway. He can press the doorbell. Ought he? What would make it the case that he ought to? It is plausible to think that we should fix on the question what difference it would make if he did or did not press the doorbell. The world will go in one way if he does, and in a different way if he does not. It is plausible to think that we should therefore fix on which way of going would be better, and conclude that what would make it the case that he ought to press it is that the way in which the world would go if he pressed it is better than the way in which the world would go if he did not. Hence Consequentialism—a very plausible idea.

I could have invited you to attend instead to any person and any act the person can perform. Here is Marvin, able to break Muriel's arm; what (if anything) would make it the case that he ought to? Here is Millicent, able to save Milton's life; what would make it the case that she ought to? For purposes of indicating what makes Consequentialism attractive, it would have made no difference which example I focused on.

Or so I think. There are other, more complex, accounts of the source of the attractiveness of Consequentialism; what I drew attention to is what seems to me to be what underlies them all.

Whether we should accept Consequentialism is, of course, another matter. Along with many others, I think we should not—and I so argued.

I think it possible that what really troubles Herrnstein Smith, and perhaps Fisher too, is that I nowhere discuss the hard, serious (nontrivial) moral problems that people worry about and think of ethics as concerned with. Is abortion morally permissible? Should we legalize physician-assisted suicide? Should we illegalize cloning? That is certainly not because I think those problems are unimportant or uninteresting. It is rather because I have not wished to engage here in the enterprise of trying to solve moral problems. What I have wished to do is, first, to draw attention to an inadequately appreciated objection to a familiar and once popular moral theory, namely Consequentialism, and, second, to make some suggestions about what we should take the structure of the correct moral theory to be. I do not think that focusing on the hard moral problems is required for doing the first of these two things. Perhaps it is obvious why: the objection to Consequentialism that I drew attention to is not one that emerges from a consideration of any of the hard moral problems—it emerges, rather, from a consideration of how we use the English word "good." What of the second? This is a subtler matter, and I think it pays to stop for a moment to discuss it.

Consequentialism is a moral theory that seems very plausible when one looks at action from a distance. As I said, it makes no difference what potential act we attend to, whether it is Alfred's pressing a certain doorbell or Marvin's breaking Muriel's arm or anything else you like: surely (we may well think) what matters is only what difference it makes whether the agent does or does not do the thing—what the world will be like if he does and what it will be like if he does not. It is only when we look more closely at what people do that we notice features of acts that intuitively *seem* morally significant, and that need accommodating in moral theory in some way. It is precisely those features that we notice when we focus on the hard moral problems.

The hard problems that arise in medicine supply examples. Suppose a patient is incurably ill and soon to die. He does not want to wait, however: he wants to die now. Is it morally permissible for his doctor to do what will cause his death? Should his doctor's doing this be made legally permissible? Well, tell us more about the situation. Perhaps the patient is being kept alive on life support systems, and his doctor need only pull the plug to end the patient's life. Many people think that other things being equal, this would be morally permissible, and should be made legally permissible.[1] Alternatively, perhaps the patient is not being kept alive in that way; what would be required to end his life is for his doctor to inject him with a fatal dose of some drug. Many people think that other things being equal, this would not be morally permissible, and should not be made legally permissible.[2] I do not say here that we should agree with these ideas, or that we should not. What matters for present purposes is only that these differences need to be attended to, not merely by the moral philosopher who wishes to solve the hard moral problems that arise in medicine, but also by the moral philosopher who is in search of the correct moral theory. The correct moral theory must either accommodate these differences in some way or show why they do not have the moral significance they are widely thought to have.

[1] It is in fact legally permissible for a doctor to do this—other things being equal. Among the other things that have to be equal are that the patient really does want to die, and for good reason, thus not, for example, because of bullying by greedy heirs.

[2] It is not in fact legally permissible for a doctor to do this—other things being equal. Among the other things that might not be equal are that the patient is in great pain, pain that cannot be relieved except by a large enough dose of morphine to kill.

These differences, and others like them, do not emerge, or anyway do not emerge as clearly, when we look at action from a distance, and ask only about whether the world would be better if an agent did a thing than if he did not. So moral theory can be informed by, and indeed, can develop out of, attention to the hard moral problems.

It is therefore arguable that the best "entry points" into ethics are the hard moral problems: that that is where we should begin even if what we primarily aim at is not to solve them but rather to find the correct moral theory.

But it is also arguable that where we enter makes no difference, so long as we remember that what we say when we *have* entered is susceptible of testing by examination of its bearing on hard—as also on easy—moral problems. What I have in mind is that however attractive a theory may initially seem to be, its acceptability rests on the acceptability of the conclusions it yields. An attractive theory lends weight to the conclusions it yields, but so also do unattractive conclusions shed doubt on the theory that yields them. What should be said where an attractive theory yields unattractive conclusions? There is no general answer to this question. What needs assessing is how seriously we should take what makes the theory attractive, and what makes the conclusions unattractive, and in what ways; the best theory is the one that makes a place for both.

Much current anti-Consequentialist writing rejects it on the ground that it yields unattractive conclusions about what a person ought to do.[3] I did not engage in that enterprise, partly because that material is so familiar to those who have looked into the

---

[3] Fisher is suspicious of the idea that the question whether a person ought to do a thing rests on what will happen if he does it, and what will happen if he does not, however far into the future these differences may continue to emerge. (The "and so on and on" in my discussion of Alfred has to be taken seriously.) Perhaps Fisher's comments on this idea can be seen as objections to Consequentialism on the ground that it yields unattractive conclusions about what a person ought to do.

literature on Consequentialism, but more importantly, because it seems to me that there is a deeper objection to Consequentialism. That is what I argued in Part I. In Part II, I tried to indicate the kind of theory that (as I think) Consequentialism should be replaced by. I did not explicitly discuss any of the hard moral problems in the course of doing so, but I am entirely happy to agree that what I said in Part II is—as in the case of any proposed theory—susceptible to testing by examination of the conclusions it yields.

2. Consequentialism

But was I fair to Consequentialism in Part I? Martha Nussbaum says that I was not. More precisely, she says that while my argument there against the theory I call Consequentialism is "very powerful," there are more plausible theories which are also entitled to be called versions of Consequentialism, and that my argument against the theory I discussed does not undermine them. I have no desire to argue about which theory should be called by the name "Consequentialism."[4] Let us for the time being call the theory I discussed Moorean Consequentialism, and attend to the other theories that Nussbaum calls versions of Consequentialism and thinks more plausible.

She draws attention first to Pettit's definition: "Roughly speaking, [C]onsequentialism is the theory that the way to tell whether a particular choice is the right choice for an agent to have made is to look at the relevant consequences of the decision; to look at the relevant effects of the decision on the world." And to Sen and

---

[4] Nussbaum mentions in her note 2 that the name was introduced into philosophy by G. E. M. Anscombe in her article "Modern Moral Philosophy," first published in *Philosophy* 33 (1958), reprinted in G. E. M. Anscombe, *Collected Philosophical Papers*, vol. 3 (Oxford: Basil Blackwell, 1981). Though, as I say, I have no desire to argue about which theory should be called by the name "Consequentialism," it might be worth noting that the theory Anscombe gave that name to is the very theory that I gave it to.

Williams's definition: Consequentialism is the thesis "that actions are to be chosen on the basis of the states of affairs which are their consequences."

Here I am, confronted by a doorbell. "Ought I ring it?" I ask my moral adviser. "To find that out," he says, following Pettit, "look at the relevant consequences of your ringing it." But which are the consequences that are relevant?

Or perhaps, following Sen and Williams, he says "look at the states of affairs which are the consequences of your ringing it."

Dutifully, I look. Having looked, I ask "now what? Ought I ring the doorbell?" If my adviser says that he has now done all he can for me, that he has nothing more to add, I will rightly feel I've been given less than I asked for.

If my moral adviser says that he has now done all he can for me, it has to be concluded that he has not a good or bad moral theory, but no moral theory—at best he has part of a moral theory. This point is worth stress. I know of no moral philosophers who have said that it is never relevant to the question whether we ought to do a thing what the consequences of our doing it would be. However there are moral philosophers who have said that there are acts that we ought not perform, no matter what the consequences of not performing them would be. Kant is the leading example: on his view, we ought not lie no matter what would happen if we did not. Most moral philosophers reject this view. They invite us to imagine a murderer in search of his victim, who will know where his victim is unless we lie about where he is; and they take it to be plain that lying in such a case is morally permissible. Many of them, however, would say that there are better examples than lying. Consider torturing a child to death. Many moral philosophers say that a lie is one thing, torture quite another; and some say that we ought not torture a child to death even if thousands would die if one did not—or even millions, or even if the heavens

153

were to fall if we did not. I do not say they are right to say this or that they are wrong to say it. For present purposes, what matters is only that there are moral theories according to which there are acts that we ought not perform, no matter what the consequences of performing them would be.

So anyone who follows Pettit or Sen and Williams does have something to say about moral theory: he says that Kant and those other philosophers I mentioned are mistaken. But he does not himself have a moral theory. At best he has part of a theory—a negative part that says about certain other theories that they are wrong.

Nussbaum draws attention to a debate in the *Mahabharata*, and suggests that we give the name "Sensible Consequentialism" to the view of one of the parties, namely Arjuna. So far as I can see, however, Arjuna's view is as limited as is Sen and Williams's: it says merely that we are "to evaluate choices in the light of the totality of the consequences they produce."

Nussbaum is herself aware of the fact that a Sensible Consequentialist must tell us more than Arjuna tells us if he is to present us with a moral theory. She says she has "so far ducked what for Thomson must be the central issue: how, exactly, does this Sensible Consequentialist perform the evaluation of consequences, if not by reference to an implausible thesis about the good?" It was on the ground that Moorean Consequentialism relies on the, as I argued, mistaken idea that there is such a thing as (pure) goodness, and its comparative, (pure) betterness, that I said we should reject it: what I argued is that all goodness is goodness in a way, and that all betterness is betterness in a way. Nussbaum agrees that the idea that there are such things as goodness and betterness is mistaken, or at least that it is implausible; but she thinks a Sensible Consequentialist can supply a way of evaluating the consequences that does not rely on that idea.

Here is her proposal. Suppose that

I have a hundred dollars. I can (a) give it to a needy friend, or (b) give it to Oxfam, or (c) flush it down the toilet, or (d) buy myself a luxurious dinner. A Sen-type Consequentialist

—I take a Sen-type Consequentialist to be a Sensible Consequentialist—

could argue here that (a) and (b) are clearly superior to (c), and almost certainly to (d) as well. But one might plausibly hold that it is not possible to rank (a) against (b), because the goods of friendship are too different from the goods of famine relief.

Very well; but then what ought I do with my hundred dollars?

[T]here is no single best choice, but there are two choices that are clearly better than the available alternatives. Choosing (a), I am choosing something that is not *worse than* any other alternative, . . .

Presumably, choosing (b) is also choosing something that is not worse than any other alternative. Then what ought I do with my hundred dollars?

[T]he Sen-type Consequentialist can say: I may do either (a) or (b), but both are preferable to (c) and (d).

However we are to keep in mind that the reason why (a) is not worse than (b), and (b) not worse than (a), is not that (a) and (b) are equally good, and hence tied. Rather (a) and (b) cannot be ranked against each other at all. The Sensible Consequentialist thus does not rely for his conclusion that I may do either (a) or (b) on a comparison between (a) and (b) in respect of (pure) goodness; he relies instead on their not being rankable with respect to each other—and if they are not, then a fortiori, neither is worse than the other.

155

A general moral theory is in the offing, presumably running something like this: if a person has an option for action that is better than all the other options available to him, he ought to choose it, and if he has two or more options that are better than all the others, but not rankable with respect to each other, then he may choose any of them.

I have summarized Nussbaum's proposal at great length for a reason. Many moral philosophers nowadays agree that goods may be, as they say, "incomparable": that some pairs of good things cannot be ranked against each other—not only that neither is better than the other, but also that they are not tied in goodness.[5] (As Nussbaum, for example, says that neither friendship nor famine relief is better than the other, but also that they are not tied in goodness.) If you hold this view, and would have dearly loved to be a Moorean Consequentialist if the facts permitted it, you would welcome a view such as that which Nussbaum calls Sensible Consequentialism, which purports to combine what is attractive in Moorean Consequentialism with the fact of incomparability. So it pays to look into the question whether or not this theory has a future.

I think it does not. We should begin with the question whether (a) and (b) can be ranked against each other. Of course they can! (a) is better for my friend than (b) is. And (b) is better for the starving than (a) is. Ah, but can (a) and (b) be ranked against each other in respect of (pure) betterness? On my view they cannot: no two choices can, since there is no such relation. But equally, then, neither (a) nor (b) can be so ranked against either (c) or (d): as there is no such thing as (a)'s being (pure) better than (b), or (b) than (a), so also is there no such thing as (a)'s or (b)'s being (pure) better than (c) or (d). In sum, if the thesis that goods may be

---

[5] See, for example, the articles in Ruth Chang's collection *Incommensurability, Incomparability, and Practical Reason* (Cambridge: Harvard University Press, 1997). Chang's introduction to the volume is a helpful survey and discussion of the issues.

incomparable—that is, the thesis that some pairs of good things cannot be ranked against each other—means that some pairs of things cannot be ranked in respect of (pure) betterness, then it is trivially true. *No* pairs of things can be so ranked since there is no such relation as (pure) betterness.

And if the fact that an option X cannot be ranked against an option Y in respect of (pure) betterness yields that X is not worse than Y, and if Sensible Consequentialism therefore yields that we may choose either X or Y, then Sensible Consequentialism brought to bear on the example we are looking at yields that I may choose any of (a), (b), (c), or (d)—thus that morality leaves it open to me to choose among them as I like. That seems a most unfortunate conclusion to have had to reach.

Perhaps the thesis that goods may be incomparable means something stronger than that some pairs of things cannot be ranked against each other in respect of (pure) betterness? Perhaps it means that some pairs of things cannot be ranked against each other at all? Thus that X and Y might be such that there is no way W in which X is better or worse than, or as good or bad as, Y? That may be true, though I doubt it. It is in any case not true of any pair of the four options (a), (b), (c), and (d) in Nussbaum's example. As I said, (a) is better than (b) for my friend; (a) is also better for my friend than (c) and (d). (b) is better for the starving than any of the others. (c) is worse for my friend than (a) is, worse for the starving than (b) is, and worse for me than (d) is. (d) is worse for my friend than (a) is, worse for the starving than (b) is, and better for me than (c) is. So the thesis of incomparability, so understood, has no bearing on the example we are looking at: the thesis, so understood, yields that all four of my options are comparable.

Let us now set aside the question how we should understand the thesis that goods may be incomparable. Perhaps there is some revision of Sensible Consequentialism itself which would enable its friends to avoid the unfortunate conclusion that morality permits me to choose any of (a), (b), (c), or (d)? We might try the following more complex idea. Consider a set of choices, X, Y, Z, Z', . . . that are available to an agent. If X is in no way better than Y, and in no way better than Z, and so on to the end of the list, then eliminate X: the agent ought not choose X. If Y is in no way better than Z, and in no way better than Z', and so on, then eliminate Y: the agent ought not choose Y. Continue through the remaining members. If any members have not been eliminated by this procedure, the agent may choose among them at will. (What if no members remain? I leave this possibility open; you are invited to deal with it as you wish.)

What conclusion does this theory yield for our example? (a) is not eliminated in that there is a way in which it is better than all of the others: it is better for my friend. (b) is also not eliminated in that there is a way in which it is better than all of the others: it is better for the starving. What of (c)? If my friend has an enemy, then (c) is better for the enemy than (a) is; but perhaps no better for the enemy than (b) or (d) are. Perhaps in any case, my friend has no enemy. Perhaps in fact there is no way in which (c) is better than (a), and no way in which it is better than (b), and so on. Then eliminate (c): I ought not choose (c). So far so good: that conclusion is surely as it should be. But now what of (d)? If I am devoted to good food, then (d) is better for me than (a) and (b), so (d) is not eliminated by this procedure. The theory therefore yields that I may choose at will among (a), (b), and (d). This is not as unfortunate a conclusion as that I may choose at will among all four, but it is nevertheless unfortunate. On some views, I ought to send the money to Oxfam. On other views, I ought to see to my friend's needs. On no plausible view, I should think, is it morally all the same whether I do either of those things or buy myself an expensive meal.

What if I am not devoted to good food? Then perhaps there is no way in which (d) is better than (a), and no way in which it is better than (b).[6] That would enable us to eliminate (d). It is no less unfortunate, however, that the question whether I may choose (d) should turn on how much I like good food.

So I see no hope for Sensible Consequentialism, so understood. Perhaps there are other, less unfortunate, ways of interpreting it. I do not see any, myself, and I therefore pass it by.

What remains before us, then, is Moorean Consequentialism—which I will from here on call Consequentialism, as I did in Parts I and II, and argued against.

3. *Moral Dilemmas*

Nussbaum accuses me of remaining "too close to the Utilitarian picture." What she has in mind is that the views I express do not deal adequately with situations in which an agent is confronted by what are sometimes called tragic choices, or moral dilemmas. Here is the first of her examples. "Agamemnon is told by Artemis that he must kill his daughter. Let us suppose that the command imposes an absolutely stringent moral requirement; but there is also an absolutely stringent moral requirement not to kill the daughter." What ought Agamemnon to do? Nussbaum says: "The right thing to say here, it seems to me, is that I ought to obey the god, and I ought to protect my daughter—but I can't do both." (She is thinking of herself as at Aulis, having to make the choice Agamemnon had to make.) And she rightly says that my views do not yield this conclusion, which (she says) is therefore a count against my views.

I think we need to add something to this story if Nussbaum's conclusion is to be at all convincing. (Convincing to us, having to

---

[6] Though mightn't (d) be better than (a) and (b) for the restaurant's proprietors?

make the choice.) For we do not ourselves believe that there is such a god as Artemis, whose commands impose an "absolutely stringent moral requirement." The details of the story vary from teller to teller, however. Let us accept, and fix on, the detail Nussbaum herself supplies shortly thereafter, namely that "disobeying the god also meant the death of all his troops." So here is the dilemma I face: (i) kill my daughter, thereby saving my troops, or (ii) let my troops die. Now the choice may look harder.

Why so? The literature on Consequentialism is full of examples that are in some ways like this one. In a frequently discussed kind of case, the Mafia have told me that unless I kill a bystander, say Jones, they will kill many other bystanders. Most moral philosophers who attend to such cases deny that I both ought to kill Jones and also ought to save the others. They say that I ought not kill Jones, and that I ought to let the others be killed by the Mafia. I am wholly in agreement with them, and I think that it is exactly that conclusion that the correct moral theory should yield. Moreover, it seems to me that the views I expressed in Part II do yield it. For it would be unjust in me to kill Jones, and not unjust in me to fail to save the others. Justice does not require saving the lives of just anybody who will otherwise be killed by others.

What is present in Nussbaum's example is a special feature not present in the example of the Mafia, and it is that feature that may make the choice in her example look harder: that is the fact that those troops are *my* troops—I am in command of them, and I am therefore responsible for them. (Unlike those bystanders whom the Mafia will kill if I do not kill Jones.) For example, it is very plausible to think my troops have a right that I not send them into any risk that winning our battle does not require them to be exposed to.

But do my troops have a right that I do whatever is necessary to save their lives? I should think not. They do not, I should think, have a right that I kill my daughter. And doesn't my daughter have a right that I not kill her? Surely she does.

We might wonder why I have only the two options (i) kill my daughter, thereby saving my troops, or (ii) let my troops die. Why don't I have a third option, (iii) take my troops home? (The descriptions of the dilemmas moral philosophers set before us very often make one wonder why the two options set before us are supposed to be our only options.) Let us suppose that further details are added so as to rule this third option out, and, more strongly, to fix that (i) and (ii) are my only options.

My own view is that I ought not choose option (i). That is because I think that it would unjust for me to kill my daughter and that, although it would be terrible for my troops to die, it would not be unjust for me to let that happen—from which it follows, on the view I recommended in Part II, that I ought not choose option (i). I take it to follow that I ought to choose option (ii).

Others may think that that I ought to choose option (i), and therefore ought not choose option (ii). No matter, for present purposes. What concerns me here is only whether we have before us here an example of the kind Nussbaum wished to give us, namely one in which I have options X and Y, and ought to choose X and ought to choose Y, and cannot do both X and Y. I think we do not. For whether or not you agree with me that I ought not choose option (i), and therefore ought to choose option (ii), it is hard to see how anyone could plausibly say both that I ought to choose option (ii) *and* that I ought to choose option (i).

I hope that my discussion of this first of Nussbaum's examples will indicate the kind of remarks I would make about the others she supplies; in any case, I won't discuss any of the others. However Nussbaum makes a general point, which does call for attention.

Nussbaum says: "Thomson's treatment of 'ought' appears to me to lack the recognition of tragedy, and thus it appears to lack an important feature."[7] How so? Thomson "moves straight way from the prima facie conflict of oughts to an all-things-considered ought, with no sense that there might remain another genuine 'ought' on the scene whose demands have not been satisfied." I take her to mean the following. There are two senses of "ought," one weaker than the other. In the weaker (prima facie?) sense of "ought," Agamemnon ought to save his troops and therefore ought to kill his daughter; in that weaker sense, he also ought not kill his daughter. What about the stronger sense? She says, "Agamemnon was well advised to kill his daughter. But the other 'ought' still remains, undefeated. It is still the case that he ought not to kill her." I take it that what Nussbaum means to say about Agamemnon is this. He (weak) ought to kill his daughter. More strongly, he all-things-considered ought to kill his daughter. But it remains the case nevertheless that he (weak) ought not kill his daughter.

I think this a mistake. I think that the word "ought" is not ambiguous as between a weak and an all-things-considered-sense: I take it that the only sense it has when used to give advice is such that "Agamemnon ought to do such and such" just means "Alfred ought-all-things-considered to do the such and such."[8]

This point is worth stopping over. Suppose Alfred has a banana and asks me whether he ought to give it to Alice. "Why on earth should you?" I ask. "Well," he replies, "Alice is making fruit salad and needs a banana, and I promised to get her one, and this is the only one available in the market." "Oh," I say, "then it's plain that

---

[7] I willingly confess to mistrust of the eloquently described tragic examples that turn up in some moral theorizing. Philosophers who use them in support of their moral theories seem to me to gain—or to be trying to gain—laurels without earning them. Theorizing that cannot convince in a cool hour is not worth being convinced by.

[8] I say "when used to give advice" since, as I said in Part II, "ought" does have another sense: we are not advising the train to be in by 10:00 P.M. when we say "The train ought to be in by 10:00 P.M."

you ought to give the banana to Alice." He says "Unfortunately, there's more: I have just learned that Annabel has come down with an ailment which causes death if not treated with banana straightway." Now what? Do I say, "Alfred, you ought to give the banana to Alice, and also you ought to give the banana to Annabel"? Certainly not. To say this would be to say that he all-things-considered ought to give Alice the banana, and also that he all-things-considered ought to give the banana to Annabel, and these cannot both be true. It is conclusive evidence that that is what saying this would mean that what I say is, instead: "Alfred, I thought you ought to give the banana to Alice, but I was mistaken. What you ought to do is to give it to Annabel."

Or so I think. Why should anyone think otherwise? Here is a familiar kind of argument. Given Alfred's promise to Alice, she has a right that he give her the banana; Alice's right that he do so does not go out of existence when Annabel acquires her ailment and therefore a greater need for the banana. Though Alfred ought to give Annabel the banana, Alice still has the right. So if he gives the banana to Annabel, he will fail to accord Alice what Alice has a right to. How else are we to describe Alfred's situation vis-à-vis Alice than by saying that he ought to give her the banana?

The answer to that question is easy: we are to describe Alfred's situation vis-à-vis Alice by saying that she has an overridden right that he give her the banana.

Nussbaum's description here is this: Alice has an "undefeated moral claim" on the banana. That is a seriously misleading description. (And I believe that Nussbaum has herself been misled by it.) A right can be "defeated" in two ways. First, a person can cease to have a right that he formerly had. For example, a promisee can release a promisor from the duty to carry out the promise. Alice, in particular, can release Alfred from his promise to give her the banana. By hypothesis, however, Alice has not done that, so she has not ceased to have her right. Her right is therefore not defeated in this first way. Second, a person's right can be overridden, as by a more stringent right, or by the markedly greater need of another. That is what happened to Alice's right. Though she still has the right, it is not the case that Alfred ought to accord it to her, since Annabel's need is markedly greater. So Alice's right is defeated in this second way.

This difference is an important one. It is by appeal to it that we can explain why compensatory efforts are required when they are. If Alice has ceased to have a right that Alfred give her the banana, then he need not make amends to her—he need not even apologize—after giving the banana to Annabel. If Alice has not ceased to have a right that Alfred give her the banana, then he does need to make amends to her—at a minimum, he must explain and apologize—after giving the banana to Annabel.

Another way to put the point is this. If Alice has ceased to have the right, then Alfred does her no wrong when he gives the banana to Annabel. (Hence no apology is called for.) If Alice has not ceased to have the right, then Alfred does do her a wrong when he gives the banana to Annabel. (No doubt not a grave wrong, but a wrong all the same, and that is why apology is called for.)

In sum, we have no need to describe Alfred's situation vis-à-vis Alice by saying that he ought to give her the banana. (The conceptual scheme of morality is richer than Nussbaum thinks.) Alfred need not give Alice the banana. Indeed, he ought not do so. However Alice does have a right that he do so, and he wrongs her if he does not. If he gives the banana to Annabel instead, as he ought to, then he ought also to make amends to Alice for the wrong he did her. At a minimum, he must apologize.

Nussbaum thinks I deny this. She thinks I say that given a person's right is overridden, "that's the end of the matter. The losing claim ceases to exert any pull." But I quite certainly did not and do not say this. An overridden right is in the second way defeated: the agent need not accord it. But it is not in the first way defeated: it has not gone out of existence. (As I said, I think Nussbaum has herself been misled by her locution "undefeated moral claim.") I did not in Part II discuss the idea that when a right is overridden, it continues to exert "pull" in the sense that the agent must make amends for not according it. That is because my purposes there did not require doing so. In note 7 of Part II, I explicitly said that in my view, an overridden right does exert pull in that sense, and said that I would throughout assume without argument that it does. I also left open there that this pull might be explainable in some other way, and that the conclusions I wished to reach did not require taking a stand on how it is explained. But in any case, nothing I said in Part II is incompatible with the fact of pull, however explained; a fortiori, nothing I said in Part II is incompatible with the idea, which I prefer, that it is an overridden right that exerts the pull.

To return to Agamemnon. Nussbaum thinks that he (weak) ought to kill his daughter; more strongly, that he all-things-considered ought to kill his daughter. I think that he all-things-considered ought not kill his daughter, and that there is no weak sense of "ought" in which he ought to kill her. For my part, moreover, Agamemnon's troops had no right that he kill his daughter, and thus had no overridden right that Agamemnon do so; a fortiori, I think that even if "ought" had the weak sense that Nussbaum claims for it, she is mistaken in thinking that he in that weak sense ought to kill his daughter.

One remaining point before moving on. Suppose that Bert concurrently promised to give a banana to each of two people who are strangers to him, namely Beatrice and Brenda, and that he now finds he has only one banana. Suppose also that breach of his promise to Beatrice would be no worse for Beatrice than breach of his promise to Brenda would be for Brenda. Suppose, last, that no one else would be affected whichever promise he keeps. What ought Bert do? We might think he may choose at will between them. But I think it more plausible that he ought to give them an equal chance, as by flipping a coin.[9] I said in Part II that if Beatrice and Brenda agree to the coin-flipping, then once the coin is flipped, the winner and only the winner has a non-overridden right that Bert give her a banana. Nussbaum objects to this idea, and I am not absolutely clear why.

Perhaps she has overlooked my assumption that Beatrice and Brenda have agreed to the coin-flipping. Suppose they had not agreed, because Bert could not reach them to ask whether coin-flipping would suit them. On my view, then, the loser's right is overridden, and perhaps Nussbaum's objection is that an over-ridden right is a defeated right, and therefore exerts no pull. If so, her objection is the same as the one I have already given reason to reject.

There is a more interesting question in the offing here. For suppose that, as I said, Beatrice and Brenda *have* agreed to the coin-flipping. Then, as I also said, only the winner has a non-overridden right that Bert give her a banana. Could I have said something stronger, namely that only the winner has a right that Bert give her a banana? That is, could it be said that the loser does not have an overridden right, but no right at all that Bert give her a banana? That is, does their agreeing to the coin-flipping mean that each has conditionally waived the right—conditionally on losing the coin-toss—so that by virtue of losing, the loser has ceased to have the right?

---

[9] I made Beatrice and Brenda be strangers to Bert since if one is not—thus if Beatrice, say, is a stranger and Brenda is a friend of his—then it seems to me entirely permissible for Bert simply to keep his promise to Brenda. These matters are discussed in John Taurek's classic paper "Should the Numbers Count?" *Philosophy & Public Affairs* 6 (Summer 1977).

Well, could it be said that it is only if Beatrice and Brenda have not agreed to the coin-flipping that Bert will need to make amends to the loser?

Perhaps it won't do to say that. But this kind of example seems to me to raise important questions about consent, and to call for closer attention than I gave it in Part II, or can give it now.

4. *Advice and Requirement*

J. B. Schneewind asks some hard questions, and I am not sure that I am able to supply adequate answers to them.

What I think most concerns him emerges in the following passage:

> Thomson labels the sense of "ought" with which she is concerned the "advice" sense. This is a misleading label. If by way of offering you some advice I tell you that you ought to sell those shares now, you can take my advice or leave it: it's your business. But Thomson is not restricting herself to this sort of "ought" or to "ought" used to give this sort of directive. Her account is meant to cover the use of "ought" with which we express the belief that there is something that you have to do, like it or not, and that your doing so is other people's business, not just yours.

I think that Schneewind is not alone in thinking that "ought" has these two senses or uses.[10] (We can leave aside which it is, senses or uses, that he and the others have in mind.) He says that seventeenth-century natural law theorists characterized the second sense or use, of "ought" as "moral necessity"; and he says that they explained moral necessity as issuing from, and only from, the

---

[10] But I do not include Nussbaum among those others. I think it clear that the two senses or uses that she thinks "ought" has are different from the two that Schneewind thinks it has.

existence of laws—taking the relevant laws to presuppose an authoritative lawgiver. I will return to the idea that there can be no moral necessity without a lawgiver. For the moment, let us simply fix on the passage I quoted.

Schneewind says that when he tells me—by way of offering me some advice—that I ought to sell certain shares now, I can take his advice or leave it: it's my business. It is not the case that I have to take his advice, like it or not. But why don't I have to? Let us suppose that he told me I ought to sell the shares because he thought it would be best for me to sell them. Let us suppose also that he thought no one else would be relevantly affected by my selling or not selling them. Let us suppose also that he therefore meant that I all-things-considered ought to sell them. (Nussbaum might have meant something weaker; let us suppose that Schneewind did not.) And let us suppose, finally, that he is right about these things: what he thought the case, and meant to say, are true. Don't I, then, have to sell the shares?

What does it mean to say that you have to do a thing? Or, since I should think it comes to the same, that you must do a thing? Clearly not that it is physically impossible for you to not do it.[11] If I say that you have to pay your debt to the grocer, or that you have to return your overdue library book, I clearly do not mean that you are physically incapable of not doing so.

I am sure that Schneewind would agree. A fortiori, when he says that I can take his advice or leave it, we should not take him to mean merely that I am physically capable of taking his advice or leaving it. Of course I am!—that hardly needs saying.

He does not say merely that I can take his advice or leave it; he says also that it's my business. I take it that he does not mean by this merely that it is up to me whether I take his advice or leave it.

[11] In a paper read at MIT recently, Dennis Stampe drew attention to the delightful oddity of a man's saying to us "I have to go now" as he is dragged off by the police.

Of course it is!—this too hardly needs saying. Does he instead mean merely that no one else will be relevantly affected, whichever choice I make? If so, then what he means is true—true by hypothesis.

I suspect that he means something stronger when he says that I can take his advice or leave it, and that it's my business whether I do: I suspect that he means that it doesn't matter morally which choice I make. But if that is what he means, then I thoroughly agree. Given that no one else will be relevantly affected, neither choice would be either unjust or miserly, and it is therefore not moral considerations that fix which choice I ought to make. It is rather the fact that moral considerations are irrelevant, and the fact that it would be best for me to sell the shares, that jointly fix that I ought to sell them.

Let us return to the locution "you have to," indeed, to "you have to, like it or not." We say this in a great many kinds of situations. If you are ill, and drinking a certain nasty-tasting medicine will cure you, I say you ought to drink it. You reply "Oh, I don't want to!" I say "You have to, like it or not." I suppose it possible that, unbeknownst to me, it would be unjust or miserly for you to drink it. If I learn that it would be, then I withdraw my assertion that you have to, like it or not—as also my assertion that you ought to. But if I learn that your drinking the medicine would not be unjust or miserly, then I stand pat: you ought to drink the medicine, indeed, you have to, like it or not.

If we are playing chess, I may say you ought to move your bishop. You reply "I don't want to, because it protects my rook." I say "You have to, like it or not, because if you don't, it's mate in two." I suppose it possible that, unbeknownst to me, it would be unjust or miserly for you to move your bishop. If I learn that it would be, then I withdraw my assertion that you have to, like it or not—as also my assertion that you ought to. But if I learn that your moving your bishop would not be unjust or miserly, then I stand pat: you ought to move your bishop, indeed, you have to, like it or not.

Similarly for selling shares. If I say you ought to sell certain shares, you may reply "I don't want to, because I like the pictures on the certificates." If I believe that the shares are about to drop to nothing, and that it is better for you to save the money you would otherwise lose, that is, better for you to save the money than to save the pictures, then I say "You have to sell them, like it or not." As before, I would withdraw my assertions if I came to think it would be unjust or miserly for you to sell the shares; but if not, then not.

I am inclined to think that saying "You have to, like it or not" is like shouting "You ought to."[12] We do not say those words only where moral considerations are in play; we say them also where moral considerations are not in play and it would be best for the person to do the thing. On the other hand, we say them only where it matters greatly whether the person does it. As, for example, where his doing it is required for his health, or for his not losing a game straightway, or for his saving a lot of money.

Another way to put the point is this. If you do not do what you have to do, then it may be that you will have acted morally badly. But it may instead be that you have merely acted imprudently. We are more likely to say "You have to" than to say merely "You ought to" where your not doing the thing would be a flagrant instance of injustice or miserliness, *or* where it would be wildly imprudent; but it is not the case that "You have to" is a conclusive sign that a moral failing is in the offing.

In sum, I do not think that Schneewind is right to say what he does in the passage I quoted. There are not two advice senses, or

---

[12] The "like it or not" seems to add pressure to the bare "You have to." Notice that we sometimes say "You ought to, like it or not"; here the "like it or not" adds pressure to the bare "You ought to."

advice uses, of "ought," one of which expresses "you have to" and the other of which does not.

I do not feel very confident of my idea that saying "You have to, like it or not" is like shouting "You ought to." But I think it plausible enough to be going on with.

So let us suppose that the idea is right. This has consequences for the view Schneewind says was held by the seventeenth-century natural law theorists. He says they characterized the second sense, or use, of "ought" as "moral necessity"; that is, that "You have to, like it or not" expresses moral requirement. That is not true if, as I think, we often say, truly, that a person has to do a thing, like it or not, where no one else's interests are affected, and it is only what is best for the person himself that matters.

Moreover, there is surely no need to suppose that where a person has to do a thing, like it or not, this fact must issue from a law laid down by an authoritative lawgiver. The fact that you have to drink the nasty-tasting medicine, like it or not, surely need not be supposed to issue from a law laid down by an authoritative lawgiver. It is enough to explain the fact that you have to drink it that we point to the fact that your health requires your drinking it. I see no more reason to think that we need to appeal to an authoritative lawgiver to explain the fact that you have to pay your debt to the grocer or return your overdue library book.

A final point. Schneewind entirely grants that we do not nowadays think that moral requirement requires an authoritative lawgiver.[13] (Or better, that most of us in the contemporary literate

---

[13] G. E. M. Anscombe famously said that the contemporary moral philosophers who concern themselves with the question whether a person "morally ought" to do a thing are using a term that nowadays has no meaning: she says, "It has no reasonable sense outside a law conception of ethics," and that they nevertheless do not hold such a conception (see Anscombe, "Modern Moral Philosophy"). Is that right? Can't we say that they are asking whether there are (what anyone nowadays would recognize to be) moral, as opposed to prudential, grounds for concluding that the person (simply) ought to do the thing? And that that question does not presuppose a law conception of ethics? But perhaps Anscombe

public do not, though others may disagree.) He says "It is those of us who, in the last couple of centuries, have wholly detached morality from religion and from external authority." And he asks how this change is to be understood.

He says "Thomson presents her explanations, in Parts I and II, as if they concerned concepts that are beyond time." Does he think that our concept 'ought' is different from, for example, that of the seventeenth-century natural law theorists? I think not. (All he directly says is "But I think it is not so simple.")[14] For my own part, I think it dubious that the concept has changed: it seems to me more plausible to suppose that views about what warrants application of the concept have changed. On the other hand, there is no bright line marking changes of one of these kinds off from changes in the other; so there may be no way of deciding which to say.

What I do think, however, is that this detachment of morality from religion does not by itself constitute a moral change—that is, a change in views about what morality does and does not require us to do. I take myself to be in disagreement with Schnee-

---

would say that the philosophers she refers to do not mean merely this, as is shown by the further things they say. Or perhaps she would say that this too presupposes a law conception of ethics. It's hard to tell.

On the other hand, I think that the practice she goes on to recommend is exactly what I have recommended. She says, "It would be a great improvement if, instead of 'morally wrong,' one always named a genus such as 'untruthful', 'unchaste', 'unjust'. We should no longer ask whether doing something was 'wrong', passing from some description of an action to this notion; we should ask whether, e.g., it was unjust; and the answer would sometimes be clear at once." I supply a different set of genuses ('unjust' and 'miserly'), and I invite the conclusion that one who so acts does what he ought not do. But I take "ought" to have only one advice sense, not two. I am sure Anscombe would object to my list of genuses as too short; however, I am sure she would welcome my claim about the word "ought."

[14] But he says shortly thereafter that "[O]ther concepts central to morality have also changed, in related ways." That "other" suggests that he thinks the concept 'ought' *has* changed over time.

wind here. No doubt there has been change in moral views over time. (It is disputable to what extent those changes in moral views over time are due to changes in nonmoral beliefs, and I set this question aside.) But I greatly doubt that your moral views would be affected *just* by your shifting from the thought that God makes morality to the thought that morality makes itself, or vice versa. Your shifting in one of those ways might bring changes in your moral views in train, but it need not. For I think that such a shift is itself merely a shift in one's metaphysics of morality, which anyway *can* leave everything else the same.

5. Skepticism

Mention of the fact of change in moral views takes us back to the idea I discussed at the outset of Part I, namely moral skepticism. If people's moral views change, what entitles us to be sure that our views nowadays are right and theirs wrong? Even more striking is the fact of difference in moral views among our contemporaries. (As I said earlier, it is disputable to what extent those changes in moral views over time are due to changes in nonmoral beliefs. So also is it disputable to what extent differences in moral views among contemporaries are due to differences in nonmoral beliefs.) What entitles me to be sure that my views are right and another person's wrong? A number of philosophers take these questions to be unanswerable, and therefore opt for moral skepticism.

As Schneewind says, I did not try to justify the particular moral and evaluative claims I made about the examples I drew attention to: I simply invited you to agree with me about them, and proceeded to rely on them in the theorizing I did. If they struck you as implausible, then that is my fault, for it means that I should have chosen better examples. If they struck you as undefended, then you are right, for I did not even try to defend them. I did not intend to be engaging in the epistemology of ethics, and I took it to be enough for my purposes that the particular claims I set before you would strike you as plausible.

I did engage in the metaphysics of ethics: I argued in Part I that there is no such property as goodness and no such two-place relation as betterness.[15] And I did that with an epistemological aim in view: I said that the idea that there are such a property and relation has contributed to making moral skepticism seem attractive—if I was right to say this, then rejecting that idea eliminates one source of the attractiveness of moral skepticism. I also suggested that if we focus on goodness in a way, and betterness in a way, then skepticism looks much less attractive. At the beginning of Part II, however, I turned away from epistemological concerns to moral theory.

But perhaps it might be in order to make three brief comments here about a discomfort that many people feel about an assumption I make about moral theory. What I have in mind comes out as follows. As Schneewind says, I did not try to justify the particular moral and evaluative claims I made. As he says, I merely said of them that they are "intuitively plain." Schneewind therefore calls them "intuitions." (That seems to me an unhappy locution, since it suggests that they are mere passing fancies, whereas those of us who are unmoved by skepticism take them to be obvious truths. But the locution is a common one, and we need not be misled by it.) Moreover, I did not merely make those claims, I relied on them. I assumed that a theory's being consistent with

---

[15] I am grateful to Schneewind for the suggestion (made in a private communication) that if I am right, we can dispense with the currently popular idea, due to Bernard Williams, that "good" and "bad" are thin evaluative terms, in that they have no descriptive content, by contrast with evaluative terms such as "courageous" and "malicious," which are thick in that they do have descriptive content. The special feature of "good" and "bad" is not that they stand for thin properties, but rather that they are incomplete, that is, they stand for no properties at all. Not so "courageous" and "malicious," and all of the other terms that stand for ways of being good or bad.

them is a test of its truth. Put another way, I took it that a moral theory cannot be true if it is inconsistent with firmly and vividly held moral intuitions.

But what if someone does not share the intuitions I relied on? I said just above that if the ones I supplied struck you as implausible, then I should have chosen better ones. What if I cannot find any that Jones, say, would agree to? What if his moral beliefs are drastically different from mine? My first comment is that it is harder than it may seem off the cuff to imagine a person whose moral views are drastically different from mine—or from yours, since I take it that you and I share a good many of our moral beliefs. Smith might believe that eating animals is morally unacceptable; I disagree. But in the case of most actual moral disagreements we are able to understand why, that is, for what reasons, our opponent holds the views he does, and it would not be the understandably disputed moral claims that I assume that a candidate moral theory must be consistent with. (If a moral theory yielded no conclusion about a given kind of act, that would not seem to me a conclusive or even, by itself, a very serious objection to the theory.) It is another matter entirely if Jones declares that he sees nothing morally objectionable in hurting or harming people, indeed, that whenever a person does this, the very fact that he does it counts in favor of his being morally admirable. How could one believe that? What could a person think morally admirable about hurting and harming?

My second comment is occasioned by the fact that some philosophers think that plausible general moral principles are more reliable than moral intuitions about particular examples. They think that a moral theory is not at the mercy of moral intuition in the way in which I assume it is; on their view, if a plausible general principle yields a conclusion that conflicts with our intuitions, then so much the worse, not for the principle, but for our intuitions.

Some general moral principles do seem to me to be entirely reliable—necessary truths, in fact. I have in mind such principles as that if a person's acting in a certain way would be unjust, then the person ought not act in that way. Similarly for miserliness. (Perhaps it will be said that these are not *moral* principles if they are necessary truths? It seems to me that controversy about whether a principle can be both a moral principle and a necessary truth would be pointless.) If I am right about those principles, then any intuition that conflicted with them must be false. Does any intuition conflict with them? I can think of no even remotely plausible candidates.

Other general moral principles seem to me anyway prima facie very plausible, but to be shown to be false by their conflict with intuition. For example, it is anyway prima facie plausible to think that one ought to do a thing just in case doing the thing would be 'more better for more people' than would doing anything else open to one at the time. But this principle is shown false by its conflict with our intuition that I may not kill one bystander to forestall the Mafia's killing several other bystanders. How are we to tell which prima facie plausible principles are necessary and which refutable by intuition? There is no general answer to that question more informative than just: reflect! But that that is the best we can say should not surprise or dismay. Reflection of just this kind is exactly what we have to do everywhere in philosophy, in metaphysics and epistemology as well as in ethics.

Consideration of the sample prima facie plausible principle I supplied just above brings us to my third comment. Many people do think it very plausible that one ought to do a thing just in case doing the thing would be 'more better for more people' than would doing anything else open to one at the time. At least some among them think this a necessary truth. If it were, then of course our intuition that I may not accede to the Mafia's demand must be false. Others may think that if it is not a necessary truth, then it is anyway sufficiently plausible to shed doubt on that intuition. Here what we need to reflect on is why they think these things. I offer the following diagnosis. They think there is such a property as goodness, and such a relation as betterness, and they think it a necessary truth that one ought to do what would make the world be better than it otherwise would be. They also think it plain that the world will be better than it otherwise would be if one chooses the act that will be more better for more people. The principle then follows. What I argued in Part I is that what these ideas rest on is a mistake. If my argument there was sound, and if also I am right in my diagnosis of those philosophers, then they have no good reason to think their (admittedly prima facie plausible) principle is true. I intend these remarks to indicate a kind of procedure that is available to us in reflecting on candidate general moral principles that conflict with intuition.

The same procedure is available in reflecting on an intuition that conflicts with a plausible general moral principle. If it can be shown on grounds independent of the principle that those who have that intuition have no good reason to have it, then so much the worse for the intuition. But I stress: the showing has to be done on grounds independent of the principle.

It is commonly said that what we must seek is reflective equilibrium between candidate principles and intuitions. I think that a misleading locution. I suppose that it is sometimes the case that we can do no better than to weigh the degree of plausibility of a candidate principle against the degree of plausibility of an intuition or set of intuitions; however, it is sometimes possible to show on independent grounds that one or the other is mistaken, and where that is possible, we can be markedly more confident in rejecting the loser.

I turn finally to Herrnstein Smith's views about value-ascriptions, including ascriptions of moral value. She rejects, first, the idea that they have truth-values. She rejects, second, the idea that they are "mere expressions of tastes or attitudes," or alternatively put, that they are "('mere') subjective expressions." She says that there is a third alternative, and I take it to be the one she favors. Value-ascriptions, she says, may be viewed "as forms of social communication which, like other verbal utterances, including so-called factual statements, have a wide range of desired/able functions that may be performed better or worse, as assessed from various perspectives." And she adds that although they are not objective, neither are they "negligible."

Is the third alternative really different from the second? If we are to understand the second alternative as the idea that value-ascriptions are *mere* expressions of attitudes in the sense that assertions of them have no social functions, then the third alternative really is different from the second. I know of no philosophers who have opted for the second, so understood, but no matter: the idea has a place in the space of logical possibilities.

An emotivist says that value-ascriptions are *mere* expressions of attitudes in the sense that while we express our attitudes by making them, and our doing so has a wide range of social functions, we are not, in making them, asserting propositions which are true or false. (An emotivist would add, of course, that they are not "negligible.") I take this idea to be Herrnstein Smith's third alternative, and I therefore take her to be an emotivist.

Should we accept emotivism? I think not. But I will not argue against it here.[16] On the other hand, Herrnstein Smith does not argue for it here. I am sure she thinks that it is an obvious truth, or anyway that it would be obvious to us if we were properly sophisticated and up-to-date in our thinking about evaluative discourse.[17] It seems to me no surprise that she thinks emotivism

[16] There is a large literature on emotivism, for and against. My own animadversions on it appear in Gilbert Harman and Judith Jarvis Thomson, *Moral Relativism and Moral Objectivity* (Cambridge, MA: Blackwell Publishers, 1996), chap. 7.

[17] In light of Herrnstein Smith's objections to my remarks about tastes, it might pay to

needs no argument. At the beginning of Part I, I drew attention to an idea that has now become part of our culture, namely that there is a fact-value gap; the idea that value-ascriptions have no truth-values is its most popular offshoot.

The fact that that idea has become part of our culture seems to me at a minimum unfortunate. Herrnstein Smith thinks I am mistaken. She says in her concluding paragraph that my students' skepticism, which I described at the beginning of Part I, "might be better understood as a duly critical stance toward some of the classic assumptions, claims, and procedures of moral philosophy and, as such, fostered, where it occurs, as a hopeful sign of intellectual vitality." I had said that my students agree with me that it is not morally permissible for people to lie and cheat whenever it would profit them to do so. But I said that when I ask what they would reply to a man who disagreed, they say, "It's all just a matter of opinion. I have mine and he has his, and they differ." Or: "It's all just a matter of how you feel. I feel one way, he feels another." I differ from Herrnstein Smith. I cannot myself see any hopeful sign of intellectual vitality in the fact of their saying those things.

---

draw attention to a very attractive short article by Elizabeth Telfer entitled "Food," in the *Encyclopedia of Aesthetics*, ed. Michael Kelly (New York: Oxford University Press, 1998). Telfer points to similarities between judgments to the effect that a complex dish tastes good and judgments to the effect that a short poem is good. She says that "[i]n both these cases we find people arguing the merits of the object in question and hoping to convince others that their view of it is right; and in both cases we would expect to find considerable agreement between discerning people." She concludes that the former "may be no less objective" than the latter.

What marks a person as discerning in the relevant way or ways is certainly open to dispute. But it is equally certain that there is such a thing: compare J. L. Austin's rhetorical question about flavors of teas, which I quoted in note 6 of Part I. I regret that I was not aware of Telfer's article at the time of writing Parts I and II. I learned of her article from Malcolm Budd's interesting review of the *Encyclopedia* in the *Journal of Philosophy* 97, no. 2 (February 2000).

CONTRIBUTORS

PHILIP FISHER, Felice Crowl Reid Professor of English and American Literature at Harvard University, is the author of *Wonder, the Rainbow, and the Aesthetics of Rare Experiences* and *Still the New World: American Literature in a Culture of Creative Destruction*.

AMY GUTMANN, Laurance S. Rockefeller University Professor of Politics at Princeton University, is the author of *Democracy and Disagreement* (with Dennis Thompson) and most recently a new edition of *Democratic Education*.

BARBARA HERRNSTEIN SMITH is Braxton Craven Professor of Comparative Literature and English at Duke Unviersity. She is the author of *Contingencies of Value: Alternative Perspectives for Critical Theory* and *Belief and Resistance: Dynamics of Contemporary Intellectual Controversy*.

MARTHA C. NUSSBAUM, Ernst Freund Distinguished Service Professor of Law and Ethics at the University of Chicago, is the author most recently of *Sex and Social Justice* and *Women and Human Development: The Capabilities Approach*.

J. B. SCHNEEWIND, Professor of Philosophy at Johns Hopkins University, is the author of *Sidgwick's Ethics and Victorian Moral Philosophy* and *The Invention of Autonomy*.

JUDITH JARVIS THOMSON, Professor of Philosophy at the Massachusetts Institute of Technology, is the author of *The Realm of Rights* and *Moral Relativism and Moral Objectivity* (with Gilbert Harman).

INDEX